Don't Fish Angry

Don't Fish Angry

Confessions of a Northwoods Guide

By Ken Jackson

Lakeside Outdoors
St. Germain, Wisconsin

Published by

Lakeside Outdoors

1045 Jackson Lane
St. Germain, WI 54558
(715) 479-5072

ISBN 0-9741644-0-2

Printed in the U.S.A.

Contents

Contents *(Continued)*

Acknowledgements

I'd love to be able to tell you that I did this book by myself and I have enough talent to not need anybody else. Trust me folks, it's not true.

Many people contributed to make this happen and they deserve many thanks. Some contributed with photos and suggestions. Roger Sabota, Rick Mai, several guide clients and resort guests offered their help in this manner. Rodd Umlauf contributed some of his outstanding illustrations. Many thanks.

Some folks offered their time in making this project happen. Tom Rossi gets a big thank you for cleaning up my version of english and making this easier to read. Steve Heiting gets a toast for not only putting the book together, but also helping me tip toe through the minefield that is the world of book publishing. Without his advice, this pile of pages would be a lesser work.

I must also thank the many guides who have become my friends over the last several seasons who have shared their stories, and contributed to my success. Our community is a small one and we all need to stick together to make our part of the fishing industry work.

I also want to thank Russ Warye. A few years ago he told me that I'd write a book and at the time I thought he was kidding. I was a kid who hating doing homework. Who would want to sign up for the punishment of writing a whole book? Russ helped me understand a little more the thirst for knowledge and expression can be a rewarding one. I now understand that writing teaches as much as reading. Even if it is my version of writing.

Lastly, the biggest thanks goes to my family. My wife Linnea makes me think I can do whatever I set my mind to. That is the thing that has helped me since the day we met. I also need to thank my kids who gave up time with their Dad so he could write this.

Introduction

Some people may look at this book as one long rant. It might be. My purpose was to educate and inform the general public about the fishing world and how it applies to the perspective of the fishing guide. Somewhere along the way I started pointing fingers and making suggestions. Our world of fishing could use changes, but only subtle ones. It is a great industry and filled with smart, hardworking people. I am lucky to be a part of it.

This book does spend some time flying off the handle but it tries to do it in a humorous way. If you ask some of the people who know me, they'll tell you that I am a bit twisted. Who knows, this book might even be used at a hearing that tries to determine my competency. The court will read these pages and decide this was the point when Jackson started to lose it.

As for the title of the book, it is pointed at the angler who has worked hard to improve him/herself and has met up with some of the same challenges that I have along the way. I hope I can save some poor guy from frustration and show that there is a mindset to being successful. Some days are good, some are bad, and sometimes it rains. It's kind of like baseball. Just understand that catching fish is only a part of fishing.

I spend a little time tipping sacred cows in these pages but it is with the hope that some of us remember to enjoy ourselves along the way. I don't have a preponderance of wisdom on this. I'm just learning that the journey is as important as the destination.

Just remember to enjoy your time on the water and don't fish angry.

Dedication

To the man who invented sarcasm. He must have been a swell guy.

Jet Skis & Other Reasons To Commit Homicide

This book has a noteworthy agenda. Mine. I couldn't keep it to myself anymore or whatever the case, I am truly using this forum to spout off and fling my opinions around like a drunken man with a handful of Kung-Fu stars. Some of the opinions might make sense to you, while some others may offend or upset you. If you agree with me, great. If you hate what I have written here, think of me as kidding around. I don't want the general public angry. I could be at a boat launch or a sport show some time and someone who read this and didn't like it might shove a broken off muskie rod into my liver. I'm not saying it's bound to happen, but I get angry enough to do that all the time. It takes all my willpower from skewering some idiot that I see ruining my little corner of the world.

Before I talk about ruining the world, I should define what the world should be. Our lakes are capable of some amazing things. They produce their own fish, cleanse the groundwater, provide a home to many species of animals, and offer a place for people to wash their souls of problems and get closer to one another. I hold my home lake of Little St. Germain to be a special place. Everyone should have a feeling about a place the way I do about that lake. My wife and I feel so strongly about it that we had our son baptized in West Bay.

Fishing angry isn't a particularly new idea or revolutionary. It's just that to many others, and me, the lake is like a church. I hold it sacred. After hearing someone who farts in church, I take a dim view along with other like-minded folks and do not want some one else's flatulent behavior upsetting the balance.

I'm not perfect and neither is anyone else. Sometimes I see parts of the fishing world where there is a good balance and I admire the way things work. There is quite a bit of that around my home waters; good lakes combined with common sense by the people on these lakes. Sometimes I see great things in other areas like Michigan or Minnesota or Ontario and I say "Hey! Why not us too?" Whether its higher size limits or slot limits or different species, I always wonder how we can make the most what we have to work with. This can be difficult with the present rules we play under in Wisconsin.

A place like Wisconsin should be a dream for a fisheries manager to get a job. It's not that easy. We have a system here where sportsmen are given a forum to voice their opinions and concerns. One April night every year a bunch of flannel shirts crowd into a building designated in each county and give thumbs up or thumbs down to a whole bunch of questions dealing with the fish and wildlife in our great state. These aren't referendum questions but the results are passed along to a body known as "The Natural

Resources Board." This board is responsible for rule changes in Wisconsin and it considers the public input along with the recommendations of the wildlife or fisheries manager. So, a well thought out management plan for a lake that is put together by a trained, expert in the biology of fish management can be circumvented by an angry mob that doesn't like it. These fisheries managers have to sway public opinion in some instances to do what is right for a particular lake. So, they are taken out of their area of expertise, which is science, to become lobbyists.

Progressive management is a good thing and in some instances, we may need more of it. I think some of our waters have unrealized potential for producing fish. Different lake users and sharing the lake can make for some conflicts and, for the most part, I've been able to keep a civil tongue and even sometimes educate those who lack etiquette.

It seems we fishermen are the ones who try to set things straight. Many of the personal watercraft users and pleasure boaters simply do not know any better and just need a friendly nudge in the right direction. Sometimes the PWC users need a shove.

The main problem with PWC users is that they are mostly using rental machines. They enjoy the sport once or twice a year and really have no vested interest and, therefore, really have nothing at stake when they spread bad vibes by tearing up a lake. The people who own PWC's are traditionally a more conscientious group who does have something to lose if things continue the way they are going. They are banned in California for Pete's sake. If we could get Bruce Willis and the rest of those crazy Hollywood types to stock some muskies and learn how to throw a Reef Hawg, we may have some new waters to fish without that awful roaring sound.

The other lake user that gets me fishing angry is the useless, brain damaged ignoramus who drives a pontoon boat around and comes within a cast length of any angler wetting a line. It seems like they don't realize they are pissing us off because they wave as they almost run over my Teasertail as I'm busting my hump trying to get some poor soul a muskie. I wonder what they're thinking as a line of 212-degree blood is rising up my face when I'm staring at their misguided party barge.

Like I said, I'm not perfect and I'm not the one who dug the lake, but really, what does the fisherman do to frustrate other lake users? Our license fees help manage the fish population, those same fees help finance the maintenance of lake accesses. These anglers coupled with other sportsmen, maintain the health of the lake by supporting habitat programs that benefit everything from ducks to beavers.

Now muskie fishermen are a little different. These are the most sincere and thoughtful ladies and gentlemen on the water. A select few will cut off your every drift and badger you as you fish every weedbed. It is extremely hard to "work" a particular fish when these specific imbeciles become part of your fishing day. I have left lakes and trailered somewhere else because of this and I know other anglers and guides have done this as well.

I try to apply the two-cast rule in my boat and I think it's a good rule. If you are two casts away from another boat, neither can be fishing the same water and there is enough cushion for both. There is also a good amount of unused common sense out there as well. Lets all grab a little extra for ourselves. As for the other fishermen out there, I know that these are the guys who need the least amount of preaching. Simply apply the Golden Rule: Do unto others and plan on getting the same back.

Winter Doldrums

This segment of the life of a fisherman has become a lot more interesting since the advent of the Internet. The old days just paled to what takes place today. In the old days, some guys would ice fish and maybe attend a boat show in January or March and bide their time away in the basement tinkering a bit. Now, the amount of shows has tripled with "The All Canada Show" or the "Chicago Muskie Show" and many others. Boat dealers hire semi-English speaking fishermen to conduct seminars on "Walleye Tactics for Tomorrow's Trophies" or some other banal subject. Internet message boards burst with cyber bitching sessions on why the muskie plug some poor bastard bought 2 years ago is now leaking water. The quality control guys for fishing manufacturers are constantly putting out these fires because now, if something goes wrong, the whole damn world is going to know about it in a heartbeat. I know some of the guys who moderate these boards and it distracts them from doing their real job. It takes time keeping some of the cyber rotweilers on a leash. An angry man with a keyboard and a modem can rip down lots of hard work with a few comments unless someone is there to defend it right away.

The Internet does offer a few jewels that can be worth investigating. Some message boards get especially spirited and it doesn't have a thing to do with fishing. More importantly, these boards provide an excellent exchange especially for those planning a trip. Resort and lake recommendations are the most helpful tool to building a reliable fishing network. This will allow you to find new water, time the trip correctly, and find recommended lodging. Planning these trips is half of the fun. It's a good way to occupy some of the winter time.

It's good to apply yourself to a number of projects over the winter. I usually wait until after the holidays myself. December is used to flush the junk out of my brain a bit and get a little objectivity about the past fishing season. I may put together a few notes for a seminar and improve my semi-English vocabulary. Sharpening hooks, cleaning reels, repainting and retaping baits all get done over this period. I try to do a little at a time to finish things around the third week of March. It is about then that some rivers start to open in southern Wisconsin and the walleyes begin to run.

Another winter project is my fishing journal. I don't keep one during the summer, but dictate the day's events into a tape recorder on the way back from the lake after fishing. I can recite more detail by my yapping and during the winter its nice to hear the details of a warm June afternoon as I stare out my loft window at a deer with ice frozen to his hairy back. It reminds me that there is a better time coming. I then transcribe it to paper when I have

A little ice fishing with friends keeps things interesting.

the time.

Sport shows are the chances us jackpine savages get to visit the big city lights and get a good dose of the insane traffic, fast pace, city water, and piles of concrete that our clients escape for a week or two every year. This is an opportunity for us to get really snaked up at the hotel bar and not have to worry about who might see us. We're the tourists and we like the anonymity. Except most of the people at the bar are other fishing guides attending the same show. However, most of the group is an unsupervised rabble of opinionated flannel shirts who can't wait to get out of the damn city and get back to a nice quiet establishment back home. So, we bitch and drink in unison. Mostly, we don't talk fishing during this time. We did that all day at the show. We mostly discuss whose room we're going to mess with that night by arranging prank phone calls, ordering unwanted pizzas, or getting into a friend's room and stringing 100 yards of 6-pound monofilament line around the doorknobs, lamps, television, etc. One thing to remember. We're all just the same in the city. Little kids in over-weight bodies.

It is also interesting to note where people are working during these sport shows. I've actually seen the same fellow working the same show 4 years in a row for three different companies. People who work in this industry get addicted to it and will do anything they can to stay involved. It can be a bit cutthroat as well. Your colleague one day might be your competition the next. It seems a little more sedate in the walleye and bass world but the muskie industry can be highly dysfunctional. I have found in my travels that three groups of people have the same tolerance level and opinion meter. Those three groups are Marine Corps drill instructors, masonry contractors, and muskie fishermen. There is no gray area. Things are either absolutely wonderful or they horribly suck.

Another good winter activity is involvement in a fishing club. If you can't fish, you might as well get together with other guys who cannot fish and talk about the times when you can. It breaks up the time some and the banquets for these clubs usually include an awards forum for the previous season's catches. Fisherman love to talk and this and it is a good balm for those who just plain miss it during winter.

Tackle Failure

Everyone at one time or another has tackle failure. Its happened to me, my neighbor, my dad, our resort guests, heck, even a well known tale of Joe Bucher himself exists where a snap opened up on a leader. Nobody is immune. It occurs for different reasons though. When tackle failure happens to a guide or an accomplished fisherman, it is sometimes a case of fatigue. Let's face it. We use equipment four times as much as the average shmoo in the same amount of time. Moving parts wear out. This is the life we have chosen. We deal with it and move on.

Another way we face tackle failure is that we often get new, untested equipment dumped in our laps and some manufacturer says "Here Ken, give this a shot and tell me what you think ..." Well, sometimes you get a new and innovative product that outperforms the old one and it's the best thing since Thomas Crapper invented the toilet. Most of the time you end up with somebody's basement Frankenstein. This invention not only fails in its attempt at replacing something that works fine, but gives you a false sense of security that this can do the job when it is destined to explode on the launch pad. It's like the o-ring engineers at Morton Thiokol peeking through their fingers watching the Challenger go higher and higher when I set the hook on a muskie with an unfamiliar bait, line, rod, reel, or leader. "Please God. Please don't let this graphite rod shatter into a thousand pieces of shrapnel 18 inches from my face ... please." I've had numerous equipment failures over the course of my fishing life. Some were clearly my fault. Other problems can be blamed on the guys who sit in an air-conditioned office designing fishing equipment and have never thrown a cast in their life.

My wife, Linnea, has endured my tackle failure-induced ranting.

My two most impressive meltdowns from equipment failure both occurred in the presence of my wife and a few resort guests. The worst one actually happened before Linnea and I were married, so she saw the werewolf before we strode down the aisle.

Don't Fish Angry

I had just finished the day's chores around the resort and decided that the two of us should relax with some muskie fishing. It had been a long day and the evening looked perfect for hooking a fish.

Once in the boat I realized my motor and propeller were stuck in the sand next to the pier. I usually tilt up my 40 horsepower tiller when at the dock but for some unknown reason, it was down and hung up. The only way to free it was to grab the back of the cowling and lift it up and then push the boat out. I moved to the back (actually making things worse as my weight was now driving the propeller further into the sand) and started to pull on the back cover with my left hand. Without realizing it, my right hand slid down on the tiller handle and began to push down while pulling back with my left hand trying to free the lower unit. Suddenly, like a muffled gunshot, the motor handle broke off in my right hand. The aluminum bracket had so much down-pressure that it snapped off.

I was so stunned I couldn't say anything at first, then a focused rage overtook me accompanied by an out of body experience as I watched myself throw the tiller handle into the lake. I don't know what words exactly came out of my mouth. Whatever I did repelled everyone from me the way a shock wave from an atomic blast emits from ground zero. I not only had broken my older brother's motor, but there was no way in hell was I going fishing that night or anytime soon. It was my own stupid fault to reef on the handle like that and I learned a harsh lesson. Don't get so mad that blood actually starts shooting out of your eye sockets.

Sometimes failure happens through no fault of the angler. Rage comes from this too. A rod manufacturer whose product I no longer use decided to outfit me with a false sense of security. There is a wonderful little rock bar not far from our resort and one beautiful September evening my wife and I decided to go work a real nice muskie that I had been seeing for about three weeks. This fish would go in the 44- to 46-inch range and I had seen it enough to recognize its markings. We both started on the deep side of the

weeds and worked the edge.

Linnea was throwing a red Mepps and I had a vintage Frenchy LeMay Water Thumper. We had just cast to an inside turn when that familiar pile of waves started to build up behind my surface bait. It was a classic moment. The cast length was good with plenty of room, the fish was rushing the bait quickly, and then it inhaled it from behind with a sudden splash. I felt the rod load with the weight of the fish and set the hook with my toes almost coming out the tops of my shoes. The muskie went airborne and I recognized this as the muskie we were after. It was the same one I'd been chasing and seen so many times.

Something felt weird though. I was distracted by little splashes in the water next to the boat. Then, I thought the fish was off. I was confused until I realized that my 7-foot muskie rod was down to about 2 feet 3 inches. The little splashes I saw were pieces of graphite landing in the water. The sharp edges of the broken rod cut the line and the fish was now swimming towards my boat with my lure and the severed line. I dropped what was left of the rod and grabbed the net as the muskie was now about 3 feet down and heading right under my boat. Somehow, the mesh of the net hung up on the hooks of the bait and the lure tore free of the fish so the fish wouldn't have that in its yap forever. Plus my Water Thumper was now back in my possession. My anger was gaining focus. This rod cost me a fish that I felt I had earned. Being the son of a retired Army Captain, I had a working knowledge of profanity that many of my contemporaries cannot comprehend. I came up with a 37-word description for the designer, the manufacturer, and the quality control manager of the rod that I had just used, so my wife could appreciate my irritation and frustration. She, of course, saw no need for such a display and suggested I clean up my language when we fished again. On a clear night when the wind drops, you can still hear my tirade hanging over the lake like a bad stench.

Muskie Fishermen Tell The Best Jokes

Muskie fishermen need distractions. After all, we throw so many casts when nothing happens that we need something to pass the time. This is one of the reasons I enjoy guiding so much. People come up from the city and we chew the fat while we fish. They tell me about their lives in the city and their worries and by the end of the day, I feel great. I feel great because they are the ones living down there and I'm the one living up here. If I had to do what some of these folks do for a living, I'd end up with shaving my head with a cheese grater and chewing tinfoil for relaxation.

More than anything though, when people muskie fish, they have time to tell stories and jokes. The best jokes I've ever heard in my life were told by clients. Because of the semi-family oriented nature of this book, I can't tell one of them. Muskie fishermen have no limits on what they will tell jokes about. Nothing is sacred and nobody is above having a joke told about him or her. Fellow anglers rip each other about their weight, their jobs, their wives or husbands, their height, their breath, or anything else that provides ammunition for a good ribbing.

The most entertaining people to fish with are cops, landlords, or anyone who works in the healthcare industry. I have learned the subtle art of not pestering these people about their lives back in the world, but still getting them to talk about the good stuff. One of my close fishing partners works as an X-ray technician in the emergency room at a local hospital. He is a great source of stories. Every week I ask who won this week's "Stupid" trophy. We secretly award this to the person who ends up in the emergency room for the stupidest reason. Some weeks it has been a 3-way tie. Most of the time it involves alcohol or drugs. I'm trying to convince him to do a book with me sometime outlining the top "stupid" reasons for ending up in the emergency room. He is probably hesitant because of the whole doctor-patient confidentiality thing.

Cops are great to fish with because they are capable of finding humor in the worst of times. They are also good at pointing out what is a real problem and what is just mindless whining. These people see what the worst of the human race can offer. So, when you take someone like this out on a lake that has eagles nesting, loons calling, and deer drinking water along the shoreline, they are quick to point out to you what a fool you are because you're complaining that the wind is in the wrong direction for fishing.

Landlords are great because they deal with every type of person imaginable. They hear the fights, the whining, the mess left behind, and a whole host of good things. I especially like the stories they tell when they talk about evicting people. The good storytelling landlords can paint such a clear picture it is almost like I am watching an episode of "Cops." I can visualize the overweight drunk guy with no shirt arguing with his chain-smoking wife about who really owns that ugly orange couch in their trailer's living room.

"My God! These Lures Are Bigger Than The Fish I Catch!"

Sometimes I really believe that people don't know what is swimming around in some of our lakes. If I had a nickel for every time someone remarked about the size of the lures, I'd be fishing out of a platinum hull boat with a wet bar and Hooters girls running a chicken wing cooker on board. The die hard muskie fishermen have, for the most part, a realistic vision as to what is out there. Others however, grossly underestimate or over-exaggerate the fish that are waiting for them.

The best one is "Do muskies bite people?" The quick answer is "Not often" or "Very seldom," then you give them a few stories of some poor kid hanging his feet in the water and having his toes bitten by some blind 42-incher that lives in coffee-colored water under a pier that just wanted a snack. Muskies have never been demonized for this because it is a rare thing. When it does happen, be sure that the *Chicago Tribune* will carry something about it and that the summer tourists will be quizzing us about the monster in the swimming area.

During the summer months, I do some seminars for the tourists to help them out a little during their stay. While I do my little bit, I show them some muskie lures and they see teeth marks and chipped paint. Suddenly there are all sorts of questions about these big mysterious fish. It is fun talking about them and getting a few new people introduced to the sport. Some of these folks overestimate what they're seeing in the water and this is an amusing part of the sport. "Egad!

His head was on one side of the boat and his tail on the other!" Or "He was as long as the oar!"

I can say that at least a dozen people in my area have looked me straight in the eye and said they've seen 50-pound muskies. Absolute garbage. In the history of muskie angling, only a handful over 150 fish have exceeded 50 pounds out of the hundreds of thousands, possibly over a million muskies, and these clowns tell me they have seen a 50-pounder or a world record class fish. I especially enjoyed the stories told by a new resort owner on my home lake that claimed to see 7-foot muskies cruising the shallows while he watched from a seaplane.

The flip side of this scenario is the guy throwing a closed face reel with 8-pound test line and a giant bucktail. I really see some folks who don't know what these fish will do to a rod and reel you would buy at Target. These people do exist and they are on vacation all summer on a lake near you. It reminds me of that scene in Jaws when the two old guys put a beef roast on a hook and chain and throw it in the water, hoping to get the great white shark to hit. The shark hit and pulled the pier into the water which left the two old guys scared senseless and one ending the scene saying "Can we go home now?" The guy with the bucktail is in for a shock if a muskie hits that rig and he has no hook setting power, no line durability, and no drag system to handle a fish that would grab a bait that large. Its funny because these people do get strikes and they only come back with a fish story and a blown out reel.

I'm not trying to chastise all here because some people are truly victims of circumstance. My first incident with a muskie was when I was 6 years old with my older brother. I had a crappie that I was reeling in when a green missile decided that he wanted it more than me. To be honest, I did not have a clue what was going on. My brother took the rod and did the best he could with it. The fish won of course. These types of things happen all the time to innocent folks who were not looking to square off with a big fish, but tried to have a little fun and catch a mess of bluegills or whatever. These are the folks who usually go back to the bait shop with a fractured cane pole telling tales of the "behemoth 5-footer that ruined my perch fishing." It was actual-

"My God! These Lures Are Bigger Than The Fish I Catch!"

ly a hungry 38-incher that was just trying to eat a snack in peace.

I am probably as much to blame and as are other guides for get-
ter people cranked up about the "mysterious and elusive muskie." I
will at some point of the day's fishing show you scars from getting bit
or having hooks rip my fingers while unhooking a fish. One of my
favorite fish pictures is from when I was in college holding up a 42-
incher that had blood smeared all over it. My blood. It made a nice
accent to the grimace on my face and Sex Pistols concert shirt I was
wearing.

I have had quite a bit of fun introducing people to muskies, especially kids. I sometimes take resort guests out for a boat ride after dark
and shine the shallows with a million-candle power Q-Beam spot-
light. On a good night we'll see 4 to 7 fish and people who would
never have the opportunity to see one in the lake get a chance. We
don't take any rods. We are only there to look at them. The more people who see these great fish will appreciate them the way that I do.
Muskies are an addictive fish.

Fellow guide Kurt Justice contemplates what would want to eat this.

The Worst Guide Client In The World

I'm pretty lucky. Over the years I have guided, I have had the pleasure to meet some outstanding people and develop some great friendships. I have had a few bummers over the years, but they may have thought I wasn't so great either. Despite this, I sleep with a clear conscience knowing that each and every trip out I give my best effort and that some days are better than others. I would never name someone as my all-time worst client but I can combine all the little things that gnaw at me and my other guide brethren to give you a picture of the guide client from hell. All of the worst rolled up into one. This is the type of person that would make the most passionate fisherman sell his equipment and take up golf.

It will start with the phone call. He is looking for a guide and wants to fish for several species the same day and wants to catch a big muskie as well. When you tell him your fee he will sound surprised and then say "Okay, but do you guarantee muskies?"

He will tell you that his deposit will be mailed right away but you never see it. There will be confusion as to where he wants to be picked up. You track him down on his cell phone while he is on his way up north and you can barely understand him. You are finally able to tell him to meet you at XYZ Sport Shop at 6:30 in the morning. He says okay, then says something unintelligible before his phone cuts out again.

At 6:29 the next morning you arrive at the shop, where you

pack the boat with ice and bait. Two cups of coffee later you realize it is 7:10 am and the guy is pulling a no-show. You dig through the truck and pull out his cell number. After seven rings a gravelly voice answers and he sounds surprised that it's you. He sounds horrible, but claims you can pick him up at ABC resort over on Lard Lake 16 miles away. You drive all the way to Lard Lake and meet him only to realize that there are now five of them. Naturally, they are all planning on coming in your boat. By now it is 7:40 am. You explain that five anglers in your boat is not safe and the original client gets angry. He claims he told you there were five of them when you talked on the phone yesterday. You then realize what the unintelligible thing he said was before his phone cut out. At this point you remind him that you were going to meet an hour and ten minutes earlier at a location 16 miles away. This shuts him up for about ten minutes.

After much discussion amongst the hung over crew, they decide to fish in shifts. Your main man goes back to sleep and sends the two youngest ones with you to catch "whatever is biting." The rest of the group either goes back to bed or tries to see if they can keep down a doughnut and a cup of coffee.

On your way to the lake where "whatever is biting," you look at your fishing clients and realize that one is green. He looks like Kermit the frog with bloodshot eyes and bad posture. His breath smells like a dog kennel. The other one is smiling and quite happy. He is still drunk. You ask him about the smears of orange stuff in his hair. He happily informs you that the stripper at the bar they went to the previous night was wearing "glo-gel" and his lap dance must have gotten a little out of hand.

Once you get the boat in the lake and park the truck, you walk back to the dock and see the happy drunken guy is soaking wet. While you were parking the truck and trailer, he fell in the lake. Not to worry though, Kermit is still dry and green as ever. As a matter of fact, he seems to want to say something important. He mumbles slightly, raises his finger as if to make a point and promptly vomits on the side of your boat.

Don't Fish Angry

After 2 hours of untangling lines and getting a few bass, you decide it is time to shift gears and drop these two dandies back at Lard Lake. Kermit is actually feeling better now because he claims he's ready for a beer. Mr. Glo-Hair has slowed considerably and starting to look a little Kermit-like himself. You drive back to Lard Lake in a hurry before he pukes on something of yours, too.

Back at the resort, your main man is refreshed and ready to go for his fishing. It is now pushing 11:30 am and he decides he wants to chase muskies on Lard Lake. He doesn't seem to see the same lake you do. He sees a northwoods lake full of big fish that are starving to death. You see a bowl shaped, clear water, jet-ski haven that has not had active fish on it for over two weeks. The roar of pleasure boaters is deafening. It is the middle of the day and your man wants to cast in the middle of it.

You convince him to try a lake up the road that has no resorts and is much quieter. He claims to never have heard of such a lake and grudgingly agrees. You instruct him on how to use the lures and how to figure-eight at the boat. You also impress upon him the safest casting methods.

Naturally, he wasn't listening. His fifth cast is a sideswipe job and he forgot to push the casting button. As you see a weighted Suick rocketing at your groin, you instinctively turn sideways and get your rod and reel to partially deflect the bait from hitting you squarely. After getting the treble hook out of your pants, you ask him if he wants to fish just a half-day or full day, wondering how much more fun you'll be able to provide.

The muskies start to move some and your main man gets a follow-up. He promptly yanks the bait from the water and glares at you, asking why it didn't hit. This happens two more times because he doesn't understand the benefit of figure-eighting his lure. He can't be helped. It is up to you. You will have to hook the fish and hand him the rod.

After a half-hour of him asking why you didn't want to go to

Fat, drunk and stupid is no way to go through life, son.

Don't Fish Angry

Lard Lake, a real nice fish hits your bucktail. You set the hook best you can and tell him to take the rod. The fish makes a spectacular jump and showers both of you with water. He fights the fish decently to start with and gets him close to the boat where he will do one of two inexplicably stupid things:

1. Set the hook again right before netting, ripping the bait from the mouth.

Or

2. Drop the rod tip down giving the fish slack and the hook falls out.

Either way, he loses the fish. In his disgust, he will lay blame on all doorsteps but his own. The hooks were dull, the hook wasn't set right, the rod was too long, the drag didn't give, or any lame excuse will be mentioned.

After this muskie debacle, your client decides he wants to fish walleyes. It is 2:30 pm on a sunny, summer day. You tell him why this is a waste of time and convince him that just catching a few crappies will fit the conditions best. Well, you do well. Very well. So good in fact that you've got his limit, (also two other guys that came) of crappies in two and a half hours of fishing. You decide that you need to have motor trouble to end this misery, but, finish the full day. You give your best effort. After your prescribed time on the water is over, you go back to Lard Lake with all of these crappies.

After almost 2 hours of cleaning fish by yourself, the clients return after dinner and complain that the waitress was slow and the New York Strip was too small. You give your boys four bags of cleaned crappies, all filleted, and hand the main man his bill for the day. He thanks you for cleaning all of those fish and says it was too bad he didn't get that big muskie. You nod in agreement as you accept a wad of bills and bid him farewell. In the truck on the way home you count the wad. It's your guide fee. Not a dime more.

The Fishing Trip

Our resort has hosted fishing trips since 1921 and I have been taking serious trips since college. Here are some universal truths about fishing trips and they can become memorable for a variety of reasons.

First of all, the weather can be great, the fishing awesome, the accommodations splendid, but if you have one pain-in-the-neck person with you, the whole trip will become a huge flush job.

I have been lucky enough when taking these trips. I fish with many different people, but usually the same core group goes. We know what to expect from one another. We know what food to bring, what we like to drink, what movies we watch, (often we bring a television and a VCR to watch in the evening), and what types of fish we like to seek out.

I have, however, seen the dark side when some of the groups come to the resort. There may be one lazy slug who doesn't help with dishes, or borrows everyone else's things. Some guys get away from their wives and drink like it's the dawn of the Apocalypse. It's always a drag to have to wet nurse someone to whom the trip matters little.

It is always a treat to travel with my group because they are all good fishermen and some are excellent. They are not afraid to try new things and they can catch more than one kind of fish. We also know what to expect from one another.

When I'm fishing new water I always talk to a local or even hire a guide myself. This cuts down on a lot of searching and clues me in to what I need to look for fish-wise to be successful on my trip. I really enjoyed the first time I hired a guide in Canada and it was a memorable experience. I had called the lodge owner months in advance and told him our group needed a muskie guide and a walleye guide. He assured me that he would guide for muskie and that a very qualified walleye guide would join.

Once we arrived our host said that he ran into some unforeseen problems and that a young man named Graham would take us out. I figured, no problem, and planned on meeting him with my muskie partner the next morning. Graham showed up the next morning and he was not what I had pictured. He was a thin 19-year-old kid with short bleached hair, Oakley sunglasses with white frames, and drove a beat-to-snot Lund which looked like it had been pushed off a cliff. If I remember correctly, I think he had an earring too. He looked like he was straight out of a Mountain Dew commercial.

We shook hands on the dock and I suggested we take one of our boats (We had decked out Rangers at the time). He agreed and I told him to grab his tackle and toss it in our boat. He promptly grabbed a small Tupperware container with six baits in it and one casting rod. My partner, Rob, and I looked at each other and wondered what we had signed up for.

"Wow, you guys got a lotta tackle, eh?" Graham said as he climbed into Rob's big boat. Between Rob and I we had conservatively 200 baits in the boat with us and another 200 left on shore. We packed 3 big Lakewood Musky Monsters with us along with leaders, 9 rods, lunch and all the trimmings. Graham looked a little lost amongst all our equipment. Perhaps a little intimidated as well.

We arrived at the first spot and I can't say I was too excited. We pulled off a section of moving river water into a bay. The green algae was thick enough to walk on. We started pitching baits at the shoreline when Graham got a backlash. Now, I'm no machine and I'll never say that these things don't happen to me, but this guy was working on this same snarl for ten minutes. I started to wonder what he had back there when I took a peek. I said "let me have a try at that one." Graham handed me the rod and 30 seconds

Remember to enjoy your destination as well as the fishing experience.

The Fishing Trip

later I had the snarl out pretty easy. "Thanks, eh?" Graham said.

I wondered how many muskies this kid had caught, but figured I'd better set him at ease a little, otherwise we weren't going to do very well.

"Look Graham, we're going to be here all week so we don't need to catch a fish today to be successful. Just show us some good spots and we'll be able to fish these areas all week, ok?"

"No problem, eh," replied our surfer dude guide. He seemed to relax after I said that and wouldn't you know, two spots later my partner Rob convinced a 30-incher to hit at the boat.

We unhooked the little squirt and got a follow from an upper-40-inch fish at the next spot. Things progressed nicely throughout the day and by the end we had a 35- and 42-incher in the boat and had follows from eleven fish including two over 30 pounds.

The week ended off super for us. Our group caught eleven

Shore lunch is a special treat.

muskies total with three exceeding 30 pounds. Two of the largest fish came from a spot that Graham showed us.

The point of this story is that a guy with not a lot of experience or even outstanding fishing skills can do a great job if he is simply on quality water. Plus, Graham didn't hold anything back. He showed us good places to fish and we took good care of him in return. I'd like to think that, maybe, he learned a few things from us that day as well.

Last time I was up around Graham's neck of the woods I asked if he was still around. One of the locals replied that he was a pilot now and was taking people on day trips to remote lakes in Northern Ontario. I hope the plane he flies is in better shape than his boat.

The Challenges
Of Television
& Fishing

A few years ago a gentleman whose family came to our resort asked if I'd be interested in helping him shoot some segments for a television show. Being somewhat of an egomaniac, I agreed. I had helped out on a couple of other shows, Gillespie's Waters & Woods and Discover Wisconsin, so I thought I was ready to produce my own segments. I had a lot to learn.

Scheduling a shoot to coincide with available crew help, ideal lighting conditions, good shooting weather, and deadlining in time for it to appear on the air on time were tremendous challenges. Oh, by the way, the fish better be biting or the tape you're shooting is going to make the viewers change the channel to Spongebob Squarepants instead.

When we finally aired eight months after we started the project, I watched in amazement as "Midwest Adventures" was broadcast and some of my stuff hit the airwaves. The show is the joint effort of about 6 men and some understanding wives, who have put up with some heavy travel. My wife is included.

Its rewarding to have someone come up and say they liked something you did on the air but sometimes the greatest feeling is just finishing a segment when you think that you'll never be able to.

I remember looking into the camera while releasing a muskie and noticing that the lens having a slight jiggle to it. Our cameraman Rick Mai was in deep hypothermia while my own teeth chattered. We had completed a fishing bit during November and both of us thought we were going to have fingers amputated because of the cold. But, the muskies were biting, so we kept on going. We both knew that if the fish were hitting, we couldn't let a thing like freezing to death bother us.

Wind is also a lot of fun too. Our show we did in the Hayward area with guide Dave Dorazio turned sour when a bit of a breeze came up. The Chippewa Flowage looked like the North Sea that gray spring afternoon. We tried to use some islands for shelter but there were many places we had to cross that were wide open to get from one place to another. The spray was hitting us in the face so hard it felt like little rocks on our cheeks. During one of the trips across the swells, my entire boat went airborne and came down hard as Dave was bounced in his seat. When he landed, he told me he came down on a part of his anatomy that wasn't designed for landing on. While wincing the remainder of the way back to Herman's Landing, Dave suggested we dock for the day and go in to eat cheeseburgers, so he could talk me out of fishing any more. The Hayward radio station reported 48 mph winds throughout the day. We were silly for even trying.

Water can affect equipment as well. I've never committed homicide, but if I could have found someone to blame for this one, it would have been a no-brainer.

Steve Heiting and I teamed up to shoot some muskie video and hit pay dirt on the second spot of the morning. Three twitches after my Reef Hawg hit the water a nice gray missile chomped down and went so high in the air I thought he had a rocket up it's ass. Steve grabbed the camera and started shooting tape as the fish went through its boat side gyrations. It looked like it was hooked well, so I let it jump a few times before unhooking him and doing my shtick in front of the camera. I checked the video in the boat after we released this handsome 45-inch muskie and Steve had done a splendid job. The framing was good, focus excellent, and the action from the fish was captured perfectly. We high-fived each other and fished on. We had a segment with a fish. The pressure was off.

The rest of the day was pretty uneventful. We saw many more fish but they just did not want to hit. The weather turned sour by the end of the day with heavy winds that tossed Steve's boat around like a cork. Many waves broke over the gunwale, soaking the floor of his boat.

We didn't shoot any more tape once the wind started to get rough. When I took the camera bag back home and wanted to check the tapes, I had no reason to suspect disaster was about to strike.

I removed the blank tape in the camera and put in the tape that contained the great footage of the 45-incher I had caught. I

Screwing up on camera can bring ridicule from your videographer.

pushed the rewind button and something sounded wrong with the rewind motor. I pushed play and heard the unmistakable sound of videotape being crinkled and stretched. Horrified, I stopped the tape and pried the door open to find the tape had been eaten. Upon close inspection, I found that the camera had become wet and moisture inside the tape housing had caused the problem. The tape was trashed. It looked as though a pit bull had rag dolled it like a favorite bone. That was worse than dropping the camera in the lake, which I have also tried. All of the work that went to find, catching, and shooting quality video of that fish turned into a big flush job. I always worry that Steve Heiting will leave a flaming bag of something on my doorstep over that one.

The best experiences I've had were by myself usually in remote or solitary situations that made me feel like a part of the water I was fishing. When a television camera intrudes, it is to bring as many viewers out there as possible. When that happens, the game show host in me comes out and it changes the lake from an outdoor experience to a stage. The stage gets more entertaining when you have a good partner. I've shot programs when it was just me and the camera. It can get boring sometimes. When I can get a good partner to bounce comments and questions back and forth, the watching is much better. The Midwest Adventures program has been fun because I've been able to share the boat with some of the finest fishermen in the business. It gave me a valid excuse to not guide that day and experience the fun that I originally sought when I started fishing. I've found that fishing can become too much of a business. It takes a little slap sometimes to refresh my memory. The best balm for that is to grab a canoe and a spinning rod and not tell anyone where I'm going.

What Would The Old-Timers Say?

L ast summer when I was speeding down the lake to a weedbed during a muskie outing, I thought about the predecessors that fished in my family and their reaction to the typical day on the water for me.

To start the day, I back in an 18-foot boat with a 150-hp motor with a $29,000 truck. I use a graph which is hooked up to satellites that orbit the earth and can tell me if there are fish under the boat along with water temperature, speed, and depth. I cast a $20 bait with a $220 rod outfitted with a $190 reel spooled with a spectron fiber line that muskies can't bite through.

I have a net that a 3rd grader would fit into and all of the muskies that come into my boat are released. Based on this, a normal person would think I have a screw loose. My grandpa Art Jackson, who guided from about 1904 to 1952, would most likely have sent me to a sanitarium. I think my boat today is faster than just about all of his cars were. It is so very different now.

Take a look at our boat launches today. Double wide ramps with multiple loading piers and paved parking areas. The old boats could be carried by two men down a steep embankment and put in quickly.

I try to compare everything. Look at the minnow buckets, hooks, leaders, stringers, and trailers. Just look at how much better things are today.

I am lucky for a number of reasons. One of the best reasons is that every year I get to rub elbows with and fish with resort guests who fished with both my Dad and my Grandpa. My fishing experiences began back in the 70's. So, when some of these guests talk about the old days and the challenges that they faced, I get a real kick out of it. Also, they tell some amazing stories about the way things used to be. Ron Gescheidler, who fished with my whole family, is an interesting man to cast with. He remembers the old wooden boats, cotton line, and pistols that were used to subdue muskies in the old days. Don Boak is another resort guest cut from the old fabric. He remembers the good old days when the true fishermen would row the boat from place to place and have

Bob Davis (left) and the author with Bob's 40-incher. Bob, a guest of Jackson's Lakeside Cottages for 50 years, has caught muskies with three generations of Jackson guides, including Ken's grandfather and father.

scars on their knuckles from reel handles when big fish struck. Guys like this make it fun for me to fish because they remember just how different things were. I try to imagine using those old split bamboo rods and wooden boats with 3 hp motors (if they had any motor) and wonder how they caught as many fish as they did. These folks are important to the sport up here in one big respect. They are part of the original reason people started vacationing in our area in the first place. Before Pumpkinfest, Colorama, and Watermelon Days there was this special group of lakes. These lakes are still the reason people come up here. The shorelines are changing and the people use the lakes for different

reasons. But, if we can restore and maintain our lakes in the way they were back when the loggers were still using axes, we will always be able to offer a special treat to future generations of Gescheidlers and Boaks.

Grandfather Art Jackson (left) and resort guest Ken Donoho with a 42-incher in 1950.

Messing With The Tourists

This is a sport all by itself, apart from fishing. Aside from the obvious fun points, the tourist is our guest and it is up to us to keep them entertained. We can do this quite easily by dealing with the day to day life here in the northwoods. We don't do this to be malicious or mean. I really think that most of the folks who come up here to visit think we have a screw loose. An example of this is when we discuss ice fishing.

When we describe ice thickness and how it applies to what we can get away with, they seem fascinated. "What the hell do you mean you drive on the lake?!?" Asks a man from the Chicago area. When we explain that 12 inches of good solid ice can hold a pick-up truck he thinks that we have a death wish for even finding that out. Heck, we can stand on 2 inches and that is barely thicker than the cubes clinking around in his glass of Johnny Walker Red. Then to top it off, most of us have fallen through the ice at some point and we laugh it off as an inconvenience to our fishing day. This is when the guy with the Red Label spits up his drink while listening.

The trouble is, when you're telling the truth, they think you're lying. What's worse is when you're lying and they take it as gospel.

True messing with the tourists is when you can assemble an entire dozen kids with gunny sacks and sticks and prepare for a good snipe hunt. I especially enjoy this one because I can even get a few parents on this one. I point them to an area map and show them "Snipe Lake." I explain that the DNR used that lake to raise snipes back in the 1950's when they had a snipe-rearing program.

After a season they would then be released into the wild.

Real messing is talking about "Big Elmer," the muskie over on the Lang Bar and the old man that fought it to the edge of cardiac arrest on a hot summer evening so many years ago.

How about the muskie that cruised by the public swimming area that ate the poor woman's dog in front of an entire Boy Scout troop that was enjoying a swimming outing? That one has witnesses.

Would you believe that some kids have a tough time figuring out the difference between the cry of a loon and the howl of a wolf? Those people exist. Who am I to ruin a good thing by setting them straight right away?

It's all about perspective as far as I'm concerned. People come up here to meet characters and get a taste of the local nuances. Why deny these good people what they really want? They want storytellers and fables of big fish and huge bears and tremendous whitetail bucks. They want to hear these stories from hairy bearded men with sharp knives and quick jokes that you can't remember because they come so fast. The more flannel shirts and heavy boots they wear, all the better. This is what Santa Claus does during the summer months. He rows around an old boat telling fish stories and cooking shore lunches.

Hosing &
How It Applies
To Fishing

Guys like me can get bored pretty easily. Take for instance a fishing buddy who gets a flag to go up on a tip-up during an early winter outing. First reaction might be to grab a minnow bucket and walk out there with him. But, you hesitate and pretend like you're busy and wait for him to get about 100 feet away from you when you quietly lay a bottle rocket on the ice, point it at him, and light it.

This wasn't done to be mean or try to hurt your partner; it was done just to see if he is as sharp as he always claims to be. If it explodes eleven inches from his ear and he doesn't flinch, he was waiting for it and you've become predictable. If he gives you the finger, you know that to him, you're still number one.

Hosing is a sport and is separate from fishing, yet synonymous with it. This form of practical joking ranges from elaborate staged thefts, to setting clocks forward, to sabotaging tackle that will embarrass and humiliate the intended victim.

The Spool Of Line Gag

This one is pretty simple and effective. Just take a spool of old line that you want to get rid of and tie it around a doorknob. Then string it around the base of a lamp. How about the handles of the drawers on the filing cabinet? You can make your best friend's office look like Spiderman paid a visit. I especially enjoy suspending a few items over a desk like the coffee mug or a favorite picture. Cars are a good place to do this also.

Cutting Your Partner's Fishing Line

Pull out about 20 feet of line off of your partner's muskie rod. Take a knife and cut almost all the way through the line and then reel it back up. When your friend is ready for a cast, he loads up the rod and lets her fly only to hear his line snap like a starter's pistol. His lure will achieve great height and distance. If you truly like the guy you'll encourage him to throw a floating bait before casting. If he just plugged the toilet back at the cabin, have him throw his favorite bucktail.

Borrow His Camera

You have to be sneaky on this one. After he passes out from a beer too many, take his camera and snap some unexpected photos on his roll of film. The advent of the digital camera is making this gag obsolete but it has classic results. It is especially effective if your buddy has some pictures of a big fish on that roll. Imagine his anticipation when he gets back to photo mat to pick up his pictures and finds a shot of someone mooning the camera. Or a picture of him passed out on the bed with signs describing his condition. Perhaps a shot of the facilities in your cabin, taken eight hours after a heavy shore lunch.

Disconnect The Trailer

This one was performed on me a number of years ago. It works only if you're in a separate vehicle, otherwise it ends up being a waste of your own time. Simply wait for your buddy to go into a restaurant or bait shop or have an accomplice distract him. Then quietly disconnect his vehicle from the trailer. Don't forget the wire harness and the safety chains. We don't want anything damaged except his sense of well being. Make sure you have a clear view of his face as he drives away and sees his boat in the rear view mirror getting smaller and smaller.

Animals In Your Vehicle

This one can get tricky because you're dealing with wild creatures. I returned to the boat landing after fishing to find a snapping turtle hissing at me from inside my truck. It took a little doing, but I got the creature safely out and no harm was done.

Chipmunks, crayfish, or snakes are obvious choices here but the snapping turtle is hard to beat. This has also been done to ice fishing shacks too, but dead animals work better here. Usually a road kill such as a deer or if you're not as ambitious a raccoon will suffice.

An unexpected incoming round is always a good way of being spontaneous when dealing with another boat.

Spontaneous Hosing

One of the classics involved a couple who was new to the area. The guy was a likable fellow who worked as a bartender. His girlfriend seemed a bit distant and tended to keep him on a bit of a leash. Some of the locals, including the bar owner, took this young man out on an ice-fishing trip to show him a good time. This included grilling out and imbibing in many fermented adult beverages. This quiet young man became quite boisterous and seemed to be enjoying this time with his new friends more than any time since he arrived in the north. He was also getting pretty messed up. Because he was the new kid in town, some of the locals took it upon themselves to handle this little fishing outing as a bit of a "hazing" event. He was scheduled to work that night but the only thing he was going to be capable of working was a porcelain bus. The boys kept him out fishing until it was time for him to get back to the tavern and start his shift.

Upon arriving back at the bar, the young drunken man was confronted by his abrasive girlfriend. She didn't approve of fishing, the guys he was with, bartending, or the area that they moved to. She also didn't seem pleased that his eyeballs were looking in two different directions and he was drooling a bit.

While she was tearing into him in front of the whole bar, a few of his fishing buddies from that afternoon took it upon themselves to try to smooth things over. They decided to offer the fish they caught that day to her as a gesture of goodwill. They figured this might show her that her man had not fallen in with a bad element and they were really good fellows after all.

They took several freshly caught northern pike and took them out to her car. They put a nice sized northern under each windshield wiper. Luckily, the car was unlocked so they were able to strap one into the passenger seat. While they were inside they decided that the gear shift lever and the turn signal each needed a fish on them. Satisfied, they went back inside.

When the boys returned the girlfriend had reached a crescendo with her rage, condemning all those who had associated with her drunken boyfriend that day. The bar owner assured her that they felt bad and this was an unusual day and that this type of thing was not to be expected in the future. The intoxicated young man need not report to work that night and he could sleep it off and come in the next day. "By the way," he said, "We wanted to give you the fish that we caught today. It should make a nice meal for the two of you ..."

She blurted out some comment about not caring for fish or

anyone who catches them. She grabbed her embarrassed boyfriend's arm and herded him out the door to her car. The fishing group encouraged all the bar patrons to the window. They watched in delight as her car pulled out of the lot, stopping every 50 feet or so and seeing another fish flying out of the car into the woods along the road. One of the stops along the road was for the young man to purge his stomach in the ditch.

The hung over man called in the next day, saying he had to quit. It seems that she packed that night when they got to their apartment and left for home back in Massachusetts. He was going to follow her. So much for a new life in the north ...

Those are just a few of an endless number of little pranks that help liven up any outing. It helps if it is done in a group environment, as an audience is always a good motivator. Just remember to keep it fun. You should be prepared to be on the receiving end eventually.

When All The World Is Right

"I love it when a plan comes together...." This quote has been repeated in many boats by a happy guy holding a big green and copper fish with a freshly lit cigar clenched firmly in his teeth.

I truly enjoy when someone who has worked and toiled in the quest for big fish is rewarded. I have fished with a number of clients who fit this description and have endured physical disabilities, frigid cold, searing heat, bug infestations, influenza, and, yes, even pleasure boaters, just to battle big fish and grab the golden ring.

The idea that someone can take the time to square off with a muskie, no matter what price that needed to be paid, is a testament to the fixation this fish projects in some sportsmen's personalities.

Many truly dedicated anglers are willing to use their boats as icebreakers deep into November in hopes of making contact with the behemoth of the lake. I've shoveled boat launch ramps off so I could get my rig into the lake for one last shot at glory before the long winter's nap.

I sometimes get phone calls in November from people who have never muskie fished before and they inquire about a guide trip. I usually talk them out of it. Freezing conditions and hunting for trophy fish is no way to start somebody out in this sport. I think it gives people the wrong idea what muskie fishing is all about. It is supposed to be fun, not a battle against the elements and a sacrifice in order to battle the king of the food chain. That type of brain damage occurs after you have caught a few. You don't need to act like a masochist right out of the chute. I set these people up for June when conditions are more civilized.

A resurgence has taken place in the last fifteen years here in Northern Wisconsin. Row trolling has been making more and

Jay and Jess Hines from Wheaton, Illinois, enjoy a moment with Jay's first muskie, a feisty, 36-incher.

more people successful and I truly think this is one of the ways that the hardest working angler gets a shot at the biggest fish. The man responsible for the renaissance of this method unfortunately died on the water a number of years ago due to someone else's carelessness. Bob Ellis was a man that fished alone out of a small

Client Roger Oakes worked hard and earned his first muskie, this plump 42-incher from Little St. Germain Lake.

boat and would often be the only one left on some of the largest lakes in the area. And, he fished for big muskies.

His biggest fish eclipsed 40 pounds but he consistently caught big fish every year. Maybe it is because of my father's influence, but I loved the fact that an old veteran like Bob Ellis would out-fish a young punk in a huge boat with expensive rods. It was the ultimate version of the tortoise and the hare.

I have row trolled a few times and will most likely do it more as I get older. When you pull on those oars and watch your rod tips wobble slightly from the action of the bait your mind imagines the bait wandering through the lake in the dim blue and green open. Waiting for the strike is easier during this because your mind works better while you are rowing, imagining what the collision of hooks versus bone will sound like.

There are many anglers who have taken up the challenge of this noble pursuit and the ghost of Bob Ellis and others before him are on the water as well. They all fish on the lake where the guy that works the most catches the biggest fish. It is a new, yet an old frontier and an experience that more people seem to be embracing. To them, I raise a toast.

Secret Lakes
& Other Lies

Guides hate to lose a fishing spot to someone else. Most of them get to a boat launch, get out of the truck and take a look at the lake before they remove the straps from the transom. I do this almost all the time. I look to see if there are any boats on the lake and where they are. The last thing we want to see is some putz anchored in one of our honey holes.

Remember, fishing is a business to a guide. When we have a spot that consistently produces fish, it is a comfort. We know that for the most part, we can go to a honey hole and get fish for a client. They think we are great for getting them into a mess of fish and they are happy clams. This leads to rebookings, referrals, and nice tips. (All the things a guide needs if he wants success for his business.)

Some lakes go in streaks and are good for different species. We fish different lakes for different reasons. One lake may be an excellent spring walleye lake. Another lake may produce bucketfulls of bluegills during the summer. A different lake is tops for fall muskie. We keep these things mostly to ourselves because we didn't come by these fishing spots easily. Nobody just handed them over to us. It is work to locate and learn these lakes. Sometimes guides "trade" spots and exchange information. This is quite common among guide coalitions or associations. But, also understand that cliques exist within these organizations as well as fishing clubs. If you are not on the "inside," you are outside. Being on the outside means you find out about a certain fishing pattern after it has passed its peak. You'll be the one vying for the scraps.

Another important thing to understand is that good fishermen don't like to be shown up. An average angler can look like an excellent angler if he is on an excellent lake. His technique may be totally primitive and sloppy and he could still catch fish because there are so many of them. This drives a fishing guide crazy. This is because most fishing guides, myself included, have egos. The thought that an angler with skills that aren't as refined could catch as many fish as we can is frustrating. Any guide, tournament angler, or professional in the business that tells you otherwise is a baldfaced liar. Don't expect one of these fellows to offer you a whole lot of information unless you have given them a good reason.

When a client goes with me I emphasize to him the importance of not blabbing the name of the lake we were on once we arrive back to civilization. Sometimes folks don't realize that they paid us not only to take them out, but we showed them where they can go after our day of fishing is long since past. That is valuable information and they should treat it as something that they paid good money for. It's not like a stock tip. It's more like knowing where the secret treasure is buried. Why share it? I don't. Not unless you're a very good friend or you've hired me to guide you.

I have always said the same thing to folks who cross the line when they ask where I fish. I never want to lie to you, but I sure as heck don't want to tell the truth, so I just won't say anything. It is from this secrecy that you can have some fun with folks. Upon arriving back at the bait shop to drop off a client that had a good morning with muskies, he showed the shop owner some Polaroids of the nice fish he caught. Regaling the story of the fight, he was overheard by a couple of guys coming in who just arrived in town and they asked him where he had caught the fish. "Right out of that guide's boat," he said pointing at me with a big smile. On the spot referrals are always nice.

"No, what I meant was where did you hook him?" Asked the new arrivals, obviously thinking their question was misunderstood.

Don't Fish Angry

"Right here!" Said the client, sticking his right hand in the corner of his mouth, pulling back his cheek, covering his hand with spit.

Frustrated, the man finally blurts out "What lake did you catch that on!?!"

"Web Lake" my client boldly stated. A smile started to stretch across my face.

"Hmmmmm. Interesting. Web lake. We'll have to give that a

The author and fishing partner Jim Rothing never did reveal the true location where these 10-pound walleyes were caught.

shot." The new guys didn't realize they had just been set up.

"I've fished up here for a few years but I've never heard of Web Lake. Where is it?" They finally bit.

"Way up a spider's butt! You think I'm gonna tell a total stranger?" My client roared with his answer. He had the shop owner, a couple other folks, and me in the shop laughing so hard that tears formed. The victims even chuckled finally.

The new guys were a little embarrassed, but I tried to set them at ease by telling them the type of cover we were fishing and how deep. The shop owner gave these guys a brochure with my phone number and told them that they should hire me. I couldn't take them that particular trip, but they called me up for the following season and I took them muskie fishing. We enjoyed sharing the laugh about "Web Lake" and they understood that some lakes should be kept quiet. Just like the one I took them to. A little misdirection can be part of the answer too.

One story of a guide in the Manitowish Waters area is fairly well known. He is especially secretive about his lake choices. One summer day many years ago, before the popularity of releasing muskies, he guided a client to a tremendous fish. It was close to 40 pounds and would definitely draw attention to a lake he would have preferred to keep quiet. They kept the fish in a gunnysack on the bottom of the boat. Thinking quickly, he quietly pulled the boat out of the lake and trailered his rig to a different lake that had an extremely difficult launch. This lake was also quite marginal as a muskie resource so drawing attention to it was not an issue. Sticking his trailer deep in the mud, he was satisfied that his plan was working. He disconnected his truck from the trailer and asked his client to head to the gas station to enlist the help of a guy there to assist him in unsticking his rig from the muddy boat launch. When help arrived, the fish was openly displayed so the attendant from the station saw that the muskie was there and that the conclusion could be made that this trophy fish came from that lake. Oddly enough, the trailer came out without too much difficulty and the boys came back to town with the huge fish, their ruse intact. The original lake was never revealed and the attendant from the gas station was happy to tell folks where the crafty old guide got stuck.

Another guide who liked to frequent a favorite walleye lake wanted to keep it a secret in the worst way. He wanted to keep it from his clients. This resourceful guide would take his clients to this lake, but in the most roundabout and confusing way. He would drive on the main highway for a ways and then turn off on an old town road. He then found a snowmobile trail that he could fit down with his truck and trailer. After winding around in the woods for a while, he popped out on another town road that carried him to the boat landing. Little did the client know that a state highway carried them to this same road that would be easier to find and a few miles shorter. There was no sign at the launch indicating the name of the lake so he affixed the name "Burgundy Lake" to it. There is no nor has there ever been a "Burgundy Lake" in this area. The route he took to the lake was so twisting and turning that an Indian scout would get lost on the way back. This confusion was done so the client would not be able to come back and fish the lake on his own later. This form of deception is harder to pull off today with all of the maps and lake information resources but some guides still try to do it.

Secret lakes also get to be a flash point of controversy and territoriality. One story of a lake that makes me chuckle involved three guides in northern Wisconsin several years ago. Their names won't be revealed but one of them was fairly well known and all three were respected.

One of the guides (we'll call him Nate) had fished a particular lake and done well on walleyes. Because he was working with another guide (we'll call him Ted) on several jobs, he was sharing fishing information with him. Nate left the name of this lake on a note at the bait shop where they worked and asked that the note be given to Ted whenever he came in.

A third guide (we'll call him Gary) saw the note at the shop. Gary read the note, saw the name of the lake producing walleyes, and then took the note with him, telling nobody.

After trying the lake with the information from the note, Gary realized a tremendous fishery for nice walleyes. He would not have known of this lake had it not been for the note he had discovered at the shop that was intended for Ted. Gary hit this lake several times and caught lots of nice walleyes and took clients there once he realized how productive it was.

After a few days, Nate ran into Ted and asked him if he had a chance to try out this new secret walleye lake he had described in the note. Ted said he didn't know of any note and hadn't fished any walleyes on this lake. Nate explained to him about the lake and wondered what happened to the note.

A day or so later, Nate went to this walleye factory to guide some folks when he discovered Gary's truck and trailer. When he went on the lake, Nate found Gary's boat in one of his spots. It didn't take long for Nate to figure out where the note intended for Ted went. As it ended up, Gary and Nate exchanged some notes of their own at the boat launch that were left on their windshields. It turned into a nice pissing contest that caused some hard feelings because of the greed for fish.

It is no different for professionals in the muskie, bass, or walleye industry to have phobias and fears about secret lakes being inundated by people, ruining their little corner of the world.

One story that involved a rather well known angler within the musky world shows how much people will go out of their way to find out someone else's secrets. This angler has his own television program and was on a shoot up on Eagle Lake, Ontario many years ago. He was staying at a resort where he had done programs in the past and had excellent success catching muskies and getting good shows put together. He and the crew had no more than unpacked and gotten their gear ready for the next day when word came out that there was trouble in camp.

It seemed that another guest had been an avid viewer of the television programs of this well-known angler. The guest had recorded the shows on television and put the video into a computer and had still images printed out of the areas where fish were caught on previous shows. This viewer then took the pictures out on the water and had little trouble in finding the areas where these muskies were caught in previous seasons. This guy wasn't alone either. He had a group with him and all were privy to the spots where this well known angler had stuck fish on television in seasons past.

This situation was quite tense and the television host wanted to talk to this fan of the show and get some assurance that they were going to be able to shoot their program in the spots that had been good to them in the past. This was a business for him and they were on a tight schedule. It is expensive to take the time to go to Canada and shoot a television show. Having a guy running

Joey and Bob Lauer joined the author on a musky outing that was within sight of their cottage.

to all your spots while you're trying to do a show could limit your fish opportunities and set your schedule back. He went to the gentleman's cabin to talk to him about this.

He spoke with him briefly and tried to make the man understand that this was a job to him. "I know who you are and what you did," he said, referring to the pictures. "I have a limited schedule to shoot this program and I ask that you leave these spots to me so I can do my work. The only reason you know these places is because I showed them to you on television. I ask that you let me do my work and give us enough space to do it."

"Oh yeah, no problem. Hey, love the show by the way. You guys have a good trip and good luck," the angler blathered, happy to meet this TV host.

The host of the show said thanks and he felt a little more at ease about this but still concerned.

The next day things started out all right and a few muskies were spotted, but there was much work to be done. As the camera boat rounded a nearby point, they spotted a boat working an area that they planned on hitting. Yep. Mr. Computer Picture Man was working the spot. Annoyed, the TV host headed up the lake and decided to work another area.

Taping was going slow and the crew realized this was not going to be a quick shoot. It looked as though it was going to be tougher that usual. The fish were not as active as they liked. The crew came around an island to hit a reef that had produced for them in the past when they saw Mr. Computer Picture Man again, casting merrily away.

Now the host was really upset. This guy was completely blowing off the conversation they had the night before. Besides being irritated from this clown jumping all his spots, the fish were not cooperating in general.

Deciding to just fish other areas, the crew went to work and kept shooting tape and the host kept at it with little success. Working their way back to camp they decided to hit a favorite weedbed where they had done well in the past. Once again, their nemesis with the pictures was working one of their areas that he had seen on TV.

The host blew his lid. He put the tackle away, fired up the engine and proceeded to burn almost half a tank of gas running as far away as possible from the area they had fished. The high performance boat raced between the islands so they could get as far away from this annoyance as possible. It forced them to fish unfamiliar water more that week, burn more gas, and, likely boat fewer muskies. The job that he had done on previous shows had been overly effective. He had showed one viewer too much.

Most of the biggest names in the fishing industry, whether it is in television, magazines, or even radio, like to talk about "how to" subjects and not as much about "where to." The reason for this is they do not want to have some of their favorite places screwed up by a bunch of fisherman who do not necessarily have the best interests of the lake in mind. I'm just as guilty of this when I consider a body of water that I want to keep quiet. If I show a small lake on television, and it's a good day on the water, it can bring a batch of anglers up that can subject the lake to possible overharvest.

I'm not talking about Saginaw Bay, or Mille Lacs, or the Wisconsin River. I'm talking about smaller lakes that can be as small as 250 acres or as big as 40,000 acres that they regard as "their" water. They feel that a particular "bite" could be affected by more folks fishing. Whether or not this fear is real or imagined, it affects the way they discuss things with other anglers and quite frankly, honesty flies right out the window. The timing of trips, who goes along, and the length of a stay is all subject to the "need to know basis."

If you're not actually on the trip, you don't need to know.

When many of these folks take fishing trips, they are somewhat vague about the destination with folks prior to when they leave. They need to explain their absence so they talk about a nephew's graduation, a business trip, or a wedding they need to attend. Then you sometimes realize that their nephew is eight, they have no business, or they wouldn't be caught dead attending a wedding during fishing season.

The best thing to do for lying about where you are going is to tell them the name of a huge lake that is near where you are going. Tell the guys at work that you're going to stay on Lake of the Woods but you're actually fishing for northern pike on nearby Caliper Lake. Hey, at least it is still in Ontario.

The only trouble with this is that most of these guys have a tough time keeping all of their lies straight. When a guide or a professional in the business tells somebody a lake name, they remember it and it is burned into their brain. If their reputation as a fisherman is good, a lake name is not something that people blow off. If this subject ever comes up again, and the name of the lake is different, trust me, they know that something is amiss. When someone does this on a consistent basis, it is best to simply change the name of the lake to something totally different. Clear Lake becomes Carson Lake. Moccasin Lake becomes Beaver Lake. Or, just do what I do. Try not to lie or tell the truth. Then you don't have to remember anything.

Overstudied, Overanalyzed & Overfed

I have a pretty good collection of books and magazines. They began with the things my Dad handed down to me. I now keep my eyes out for new books and am always looking for special books that either outline tactics or books that deal with new fisheries and areas to try an experience.

Many of the books from 50 and 60 years ago were great to read, but they were usually written by a columnist or outdoor writer who was a visitor to the woods and didn't have a great first hand knowledge of fishing or hunting. They enlisted the help of guides or local anglers and passed off second hand information. It wasn't as informative for a couple of reasons. First, I think some things were lost in the translation and second, I don't think the guides trusted him and didn't tell the writer everything they could have.

In the 1970's some anglers with great knowledge and innovation began to communicate their tactics and methods from a first-hand level and moved the skill level of the average fisherman up several notches quite quickly.

In-Fisherman, Fishing Facts, and several other publications dealt with tactics and detailed ways of catching more fish. Towards the end of the 1970's and early 1980's mapping companies and other enterprises packaged information to help anglers find fish. Fishing Hot Spots was one of these companies. It produced books and individual lake maps that revealed stocking information, lake history, and management practices and how it related to the fishery. The quality of the information that was being circulated improved tremendously. Coverage was widespread and people were learning about ways of catching fish and learning new lakes faster than any time before.

Somewhere along the way, somebody started to make a little money in this business. When that happened, many more folks jumped into the fray. It included the production of television shows, sport and trade shows, new magazines, fishing schools, and videos featuring fishing and an assortment of other outdoor subjects. Some projects were dedicated solely to one specific species of fish. New tackle was on the way as well. Everything improved except for the lakes and the fish. They stayed pretty much the same.

Now with this renaissance of information, there was bound to be some bad information. Anybody with a typewriter could blast out an article, submit it to an editor, and if it passed muster, get published as fact. The problem was that some editors were not as sharp at weeding out the crap that ended up making it in print. Some projects floundered while others gained strength and produced quality information to the angler who had a thirst for information.

Another problem that has cropped up is a "second generation" of fishing information experts. These are disciples of the initial group of information experts that have taken the torch of communicating fishing tactics and methods. Many have been excellent at refining skills that were pioneered by others. Some however, have simply repackaged old information and claimed it as their own. Now, it seems like anybody who has caught a 45-inch muskie is qualified to write an article and become a guide. This is a growing segment of the fishing industry and has created a discernable gray area as to who is an expert and who pretends to be one. This is also a reason some fishing information that comes out in print and on the Internet is questionable. Some bad advice has seen the light of day. Some anglers have political views and axes to grind that use the Internet to voice their opinions. Some of the opinions have to do with management of the fisheries, other anglers, and ethics within the sport. This extra fat that has to be trimmed crowds out some of the good information, making it tougher to find the "good stuff."

Muskie anglers are as zealous a group as you will find. They will spend large amounts of money to get any kind of edge they can so they will be a better position to catch fish. It is this search for the Holy Grail of information that will confuse more anglers than it will help.

Allow me to amaze and confuse you with techniques and tactics that will leave you with more questions than answers.

Overstudied, Overanalyzed & Overfed

Have you heard the saying that you can find anything you want in the Bible if you look hard enough? The same thing goes for fishing tactics. You can find contradictions everywhere as far as tactics go and nobody could be considered wrong. For an article that says throw small baits for muskies in spring, I can dig one up that says you should go against the grain and throw a bigger bait to get their attention. Fish shallow? No way. This article says that you should fish deep and don't bother with shallow water. This type of confusion can make a normal person ask what he has gotten into.

Well, I'm here to help. My advice is to pay attention to all of it. You should also ignore it.

Each of the television segments, seminar presentations and magazine articles you see are based on someone else's personal experience. What they are talking about may not fit the kind of fishing you do at all. For instance, there might be an "expert" giving a presentation at a sport show that deals with muskies. If all of the slides that he shows during his presentation show fish that were boated in Canada, and you only fish in Wisconsin, this guy's advice isn't going to help you very much. Especially if he doesn't tell you that these were Canadian fish. You cannot just take one set of tactics and plug them into every lake and expect them to work, although some of these so-called "pros" would like you to believe so. Remember, many of these guys want to talk "how to" and not "where to."

Another important thing to realize is that the images of fish that are seen on television, in videos, at seminars, and in magazines are caught on lakes that aren't necessarily shared with the public. These fish were caught on top lakes and in situations where the tactics may not have been all that important. Yeah, that fish may have been caught on a bucktail that had a certain type of blade but the fish were so damn active that day it might have eaten a used rubber floating in the water because the lake was so hot and the weather conditions so good. Remember, an excellent lake can make an average fisherman look like an expert.

Don't Fish Angry

I read a great passage in a book written by Dick Pearson. His book, *Muskies On the Shield* talked about how some of today's fishermen have some ideas about how to fish muskies with specific tactics, and can be successful at them. When that particular tactic they do well doesn't work, they don't have good fishing fundamentals to fall back on. I've seen this plenty of times. Some guys are great at throwing bucktails. But, when these fish want reapers or jigs thrown at them, they don't have a clue. This is a product of some of the diluted or selective information that the information hungry angler finds. It's like a surgeon that knows how to do heart bypass but can't perform CPR. They have gotten ahead of themselves.

One of the best ways to learn is in person in the presence of a guide. You can get one-on-one attention and learn in a much better environment. Plus, the guide can't give you any kind of snow job about tactics and location. Learning and mastering the tricks of one particular lake is going to help you in the long run. There may be situations where those tactics may work on another lake, but don't count on it.

A great way to build a knowledge of fishing is to fish with many different guides on different waters for different species. You're bound to be exposed to special tactics that your particular guide excels at. Hopefully, he's also a good teacher. This type of approach can make your learning curve quite steep. Just choose carefully the guides you hire and the region that you're fishing. Then, tell the guide what you really want to learn. If you want to become really good at fishing muskies on Lake Kawaguesaga, tell him that. Ask about how to fish it during different times of the year and what baits work under the best situations. Another thing to remember is that each lake has one guide who fishes it the best. Try to find out who that best guide is. After all, whom would you rather learn from? A guide with a Yale equivalent fishing education or a Johnny-come-lately with a knowledge equivalent to Buffalo Grove Community College?

A fun place to learn is a fishing school. This is when you join a group of others at a resort or lodge and spend time with instructors both on the water and in class or seminar situations. Besides enjoying the fun of being on a trip, you are immersed into the fishing psyche and you'll have few distractions away from the intended purpose, learning how to catch fish.

Many different businesses within the fishing industry have sponsored such teaching clinics and they have been a success in almost all situations. If run correctly, they are profitable and a great learning experience for those who seek more polished skills. Several guides may be involved and a combined teaching experience like this can be excellent.

The bottom line to learning more about fishing is to simplify the method that you obtain information. There is so much crap floating around out there that it can be confusing. Find the most reliable sources you can for how-to and where-to information and keep good track of it. There are some good specialty articles and seminars out there but regard them in the right context. The subject method may be for a specialty situation and of little use except for that certain situation that you may not even encounter. If need be, ask questions and press the speaker or writer on specifics of a method if you feel he is being vague. If you're asking enough questions, you'll eventually get him to admit that he doesn't know. Fishing experts hate to admit to this but it is only then that you know you've exhausted them on a subject. Make sure you don't agitate them though. It may be a long swim.

Why Did You Buy THAT?!

I have a client named Phil. We fish together at least once a year and always have a fun time. Phil drives up the gross national product when he comes up here. He buys lures. He owns so many lures that distributors call him when they have problems filling an order at Bass Pro Shops. Every year, it seems we get action on a lure that he doesn't own yet. This leads to another sale. He doesn't smoke, drink, or gamble. Phil buys lures.

Some guys take tackle to a whole different level. I have a solid collection, but I have found that the last couple of years that I've caught most of my muskies on about 25 lures. I own over 400 though. Did I overbuy? Was I grasping at straws? I don't think so. It is a process of elimination to find out which lures work on certain lakes. The more lakes you fish, it is likely the more lures you need. If I only fished Big St. Germain, I could get away with six baits if I was stingy.

Television is to blame for many fisherman buying junk. I have seen Banjo Minnows and all other kinds of questionable tackle being peddled as the new great white hope of fishing. What they don't necessarily tell you is where the infomercial was shot. You could call the 800 number they give you and ask the operator where the fish in the video were caught. She might not be much help though.

I mentioned Phil before. Many people with less self control feel obligated to arrive here in God's country with a ready arsenal

Mike Kaminski demonstrates that when it comes to muskie tackle, neatness counts.

of lures that will slay fish. I get phone calls from clients in January and February asking what lures to buy for their trip in July. Invariably, I tell them to buy nothing and get what they need up here. This is good for a couple of reasons.

First, they end up buying a bunch of stuff that they may not need. It makes sense to get some new lures every year but someone starting out needs to acquire the lures that will work on the lake he is specifically fishing. With the rising cost of lures, it makes sense to buy only what you need. It makes sense to buy baits from a store that is located less than a mile or so from the lake you are fishing. Trust me, the people in that shop know what works on that lake.

The other reason that I recommend people to get lures in the area they are fishing is to bolster the local economy. The small bait shop in any vacation town is bound to have knowledgeable people working there. Besides, if you drop a little money in a local shop you can generally get some good advice that money some-

This is Phil. Phil buys baits.

times cannot buy. Buying a map of a local lake is a good idea as well. If you get it at small shop near the lake, you are bound to get a few spots marked on the map for you if you act helpless enough. A few good clues from a local bait shop owner is always a good thing. He wants you to do well on your trip. That means you'll come back to his shop.

Roger Sabota, one of the best muskie fishermen in the business, poses with one of his close friends beneath his monumental arsenal of musky lures.

The Dumbest Thing You'll Ever See

One of the favorite stories my Dad would tell involved the time he was a young man guiding a resort guest for muskies on our lake. During this era, the guides rowed the boat from spot to spot and pointed out areas to cast. After a while, the guide would simply row the boat and the angler would hold onto the rod and wait for a strike, trolling his bait behind the boat.

This particularly hot summer day involved a rather large opinionated man who didn't seem to do a whole lot of casting. He wanted to troll, but he didn't want to hold onto the rod. He wanted to wrap the line tightly around his hand waiting for the strike. My Dad recognized the problem that might develop and suggested to the portly man that he should hold the rod instead as his hand might get hurt doing this.

"I want to feel the strike! I've done this before so pay attention to your oars. You're getting paid to row the boat so ROW THE BOAT ..."

My Dad simply shrugged his shoulders and continued to row when a little while later the fat man began to howl as his arm jerked forward. He spun halfway around and yelled that he had a strike. He tried to grab the rod to fight the fish but the tension of the fish pulling against his hand was too great and he was unable to unwrap the line from his hand. The muskie jumped and was

A young George Jackson spent many summer days on the water and witnessed the finest in inexplicable behavior.

able to throw the hook. It was quite large as my Dad estimated it between 25 and 30 pounds.

The man groaned in pain as he set the rod down and looked at his bloody right hand. The fish had struck so hard that the cotton line had sliced through the skin on his hand like a knife into an Easter ham. The line was buried deep into the skin and simply pulling it out was like yanking out a big wooden sliver. "Give me some help with my hand! This is killing me!"

My Dad, pretending not to notice while he continued to row towards the resort said; "I'm not sure how to help. I'm just getting paid to row the boat ... "

I learned many lessons from Dad and many times it was in the presence of watching somebody else do something mind bogglingly stupid. He would anticipate it and point it out to me.

"Look at that silly S.O.B. over there." Dad would calmly say, pointing at a small speedboat careening towards the Tobin Bar and

Dad would often hold court down by the lake and bluntly state his opinions on the absence of lake etiquette.

its rocky bottom and 10 inches of water. The bar was surrounded by several markers indicating a shallow, hazardous bottom. "His vacation is going into the crapper in about 5 seconds."

I cringed as I watched a carefree, happy, ignorant boater ram an expensive lower unit and propeller into the rocks at 40 mph. I think he tasted the windshield a bit as the boat ran aground and came to an abrupt stop. We continued to fish as I watched my Dad shake his head and quietly chuckle as we had witnessed another hot dog fry himself.

Boat launches are the locations where the dumbest things take place. I have to admit that I have a short fuse at the launch and am less tolerant than I should be. I guess that because I do things quickly, everyone should be able to as well. I've timed myself. It takes about 4 minutes for me to launch my boat and about 6 minutes to pull it out. I guess that when you do it 5 or 6 days a week all summer, it gets to be habit. When I listen to some of my clients who fish in southern Wisconsin and northern Illinois, and hear about what happens at the boat landing down there, I thank God I don't have to deal with it.

During the heart of the busy season I'll see two or three people a week at boat launches who have no business being there. They either can't back up a trailer, or line up the boat, or back the trailer in too far, or not enough. Then, after clogging up the ramp for 25 minutes, they occupy the loading pier by trying to start an outboard motor that hasn't run since the Jimmy Carter years. They act shocked that things aren't running so smoothly.

Friday nights are always good at the launch, especially on an active tourist lake. People are pulling their boats out and are preparing to pack. I remember one of the all time classics from a few years ago at the Little St. Germain launch. A fake wooden panel station wagon, you know, an old Country Squire like Clark Griswold drove, backed in like a crooked snake down the ramp. Now there was a bit of an angle here because old Clark wasn't straight and the ramp there can seem a bit steep. Then I see the USS Yorktown pull up to the launch. A beast of a Boston Whaler that had to weigh 4,000 pounds. It took about 15 minutes to get it on the bunks right and the bow cranked up tight. We were ready for the big moment. It was time to yank it out.

The driver hit the gas and in 30 seconds I watched 20,000 miles of rear tire tread melt away in a cloud of blue smoke. The tires spun so wild and hot that the EPA was called in to measure the pollution index from the fire inside the wheel wells. The ship rose slowly out of the lake and picked up speed as the Country Squire straightened out and aimed its way back up the road towards the parking area. Just as the motor found its way out of the lake the lower unit of the engine struck the pavement and started to plow a furrow in the asphalt. They neglected to tilt the motor up and now it was stuck. This stopped the ascent and forced Mr. Griswold to a halt.

One of the guys standing at the launch offered to help try to tilt the motor up while the boat was pulled forward. After 10 more minutes, the motor was up and the big Whaler was pulled the rest of the way up the road. The smell of barbequed clutch and burnt tire hung in the air for more than an hour. The skid marks on the launch lasted for several summers until time washed them away.

Guides are capable of performing dumb things on the water as

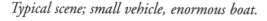

Typical scene; small vehicle, enormous boat.

The Dumbest Thing You'll Ever See

well. Jim Santefort, a retired police officer that lives in my hometown, traveled to Ontario for a walleye trip several years ago and had an interesting experience involving the guide from his camp.

They met on the dock in the morning and were introduced by the camp owner. The guide was a member of the local Indian tribe and while not being a gregarious fellow, was still thought of as a good walleye guide.

Jim loaded quite a bit of tackle and equipment into the boat and the guide seemed unfamiliar with some of the things Jim had packed. They fired up the boat and took off up the lake towards their first spot of the morning. While on the way to the spot, the guide yelled over the drone of the outboard motor to Jim and he seemed confused. Sitting in the middle seat, Jim turned towards the back of the boat to see the Indian man with a pair of jaw spreaders in his hand. These are commonly used for helping unhook deeply hooked fish by preventing the mouth from closing. They are made from wire that is similar to what you'll see in a coat hanger. They are spring loaded and quite effective at keeping the jaws of even powerful fish wide open. Obviously, the guide was unfamiliar with them.

"Jaw spreaders!" Jim yelled over the sound of the outboard. The guide still seemed confused. "Holds the fish's mouth open!" Jim bellowed over the engine noise. The guide still looked perplexed so Jim motioned to his mouth and pretended to squeeze the jaw spreaders open. The guide nodded that he understood and Jim turned around to face the bow and take in the view before him as they continued on towards their first walleye spot of the morning.

Suddenly, the boat took a sharp angle as tackle boxes tipped and Jim nearly fell from his seat in the boat. The boat was nearly on its side when Jim whirled around to the back to see what happened in the back to cause such a turn that nearly flipped them over.

The guide was howling in pain as Jim saw the jaw spreaders wedged tightly against the lips of their boat pilot. It seemed that

Don't Fish Angry

Jim wasn't specific about the jaw spreaders being for the fish. Somehow, the guide seemed to think he needed to try them out personally. The guide regained control of the boat and Jim then squeezed the jaw spreaders and pulled them from the poor Indian's mouth. They had a good laugh at the end of the day but almost flipping the boat hardly seemed worth it.

What Guides Talk About When No One Else Is Listening

Favorite subjects around the campfire at night usually deal with humorous and funny things on the water. We usually have good material from our clients whether it is a joke they told or something that happened on the water. But, you may be surprised what guides talk about when nobody else is listening. It often has nothing to do with fishing.

I was at a sport show hotel a few years ago chewing the fat with a late guide from Arbor Vitae, Wisconsin, named George Kurek. We had just got done working all day at a show when we had some quiet time and we were talking about hanging drywall. The winter months are the time that we can get our honey-do's completed as the fishing season occupies us to the limit. George had this project going on as soon as he got back home. Suddenly, a fellow from out of town recognized George from a magazine picture and started grilling him about weed walleyes and when he should travel north for such a trip. George obliged and chatted with the guy for a few minutes and the guy felt like he was a personal friend of George.

"Who is that guy?" I asked. "Beats me," George replied. "I think you told him more than he deserved," I said. "Yeah, but at least he's off my back now," George shrugged.

We got back to our discussion about hanging drywall and the problems of mudding and taping before we met with another group of guides to decide whose room was going to be sabotaged

Don't Fish Angry

that night.

Things like that happen to all noted fishing guides. Guides could be pumping gas, buying groceries, mailing a letter, or making a bank deposit and whoever sees you will ask for fishing advice. This sometimes leads to a guide job, but not often. Maybe I'm being a curmudgeon, but by Labor Day, I'm good and sick of it. I want to talk about anything but my job. I love to fish, but it's good to have balance in your life.

Fellow guide Rob Manthei complained for months about the "Atomic Backlash" that one of his clients spun with his rod.

What Guides Talk About When No One Else Is Listening

Becoming a father was the most rewarding thing that ever happened to me. I love to talk about my kids. I bore the hell out of people telling stories about them but I don't care. I just think they're great. Guides who have families usually talk about them as much as anything, especially with other guides. During the fishing season, we don't see our families very much. There are many days I leave the house when the whole family is still asleep and don't get back home until they have all gone to bed. I try to spend at least an afternoon a week with them during the summer but you have to make hay when the sun shines.

The other thing we talk about is our clients and their antics on the water. We brag when we have a client who can cast well and is a treat to fish with. We complain and moan when we get an idiot who doesn't listen and makes the day seem longer than usual. I said earlier, I'm lucky. I get a pretty good group of people who I enjoy fishing with. I get maybe one or two bummers a year. If you get 50 guides together, you'll have 100 good stories a year about guide clients who should have stayed on shore.

Equipment is a big issue that guides love to talk about. New types of line, boats, reels, baits, batteries, trailers, and motors are all popular topics. Learning the names of good mechanics are shared as well. Anytime you can find a good mechanic to get you back on the water, it is important. Many guides are looking for quotes on liability insurance. Names of tackle and marine reps are passed around so some of these items can be acquired at wholesale prices. The business part of the guiding is always a popular topic.

You'd actually be surprised how little some guides actually talk about fishing. It still goes back to the cliques and protecting their "secret waters." If a guy opens his yap and reveals something, he is welcoming a new group of anglers to fish a spot that he may need in the future. It's like a social disease. It's not that you're just telling one person. You are telling that person and anyone else that they might tell. It is a pyramid that can get out of control in a hurry, especially if someone in the pyramid is trying to impress somebody. That is how guide associations and coalitions can get as immature as a group of thirteen year old girls.

Helpful, friendly mechanics are always sought after by guides who want to keep their boat running smoothly.

Don't Gag
On All Of It

Remember, fishing is supposed to be fun. It is fun to discover new water, catch different fish, meet new people, and travel to interesting and beautiful places. Fishing outings happen for different reasons and they are all good ones. My favorite reason to fish is to spend time with my wife and family and share some memories with them. It's amazing how different my attitude about fishing and guiding has changed in the last 10 years.

When starting out, most younger guides have a tremendous ego that needs to be fed by continual success. You live and die by your victories and defeats on the water, and you're only as good as your last day. You're more driven because you feel so obligated to constantly prove yourself. If you want to build a business as a guide, this is necessary. You have to prove that you can produce. It also leads you to drink more because sometimes the fish make you so crazy that you can't sleep.

After a few years of fishing in the snow and heavy winds you develop enough experiences that you can kind of tell what success you'll have before you put the boat in that day. Your confidence grows and your ego stabilizes a bit but by most people's standards you are still a pain in the ass.

I look at guys who have been guiding in my area for many years and I see the attitude that you need to keep it a fun and a rewarding part of their lives. Fishing is a sport that can numb some people because they can get burned out. They guide too much or their quest for recognition grows so much they feel they need to fish beyond their limits or financial means. Many excellent guides either never grew out of the hard drinking stage or didn't try to. They moved up north and within a couple of years either stopped fishing or fished to the point that their marriage fell by the side of the road. They gagged on it. When this happens, they lose the love for the sport that initially drove them to try it in the first place. Some of those fishermen who fished beyond themselves were younger men. It is a shame because they were invariably good anglers who simply lost the taste for it.

There is also a difference in the way guides earn their living as opposed to the "old days." Honestly, few guides are full time anymore and most, myself included, work other jobs to make a living. Many guides in the northwoods are or have been schoolteachers. Some are flooring installers, carpenters, bait shop owners, or mechanics. I'm lucky because my family owns a resort and I have no shortage of work on my hands. There are some full time guides left throughout the north. They guide close to 200 days a year and spend the winter either making baits or writing fishing articles. By November, these guys have had enough. They are the last of the old guard. They live a life of extremes.

A stop with the golfing group at a local establishment after a morning round is a necessity.

Don't Gag On All Of It

I mentioned earlier that balance was an important factor in a lake. It is also important for the fisherman, at least it is for me. Like Mr. Miagi said in Karate Kid, "Must seek balance!"

Every summer there is a group that comes to our resort about the second week of July. I usually spend a fair amount of time helping the guests catch fish but, this week does not have a heavy group of fishermen. There are a couple in the group that do, but not with a tremendous amount of zeal. My main fishing that week is with the Jim Laasch family. We go after muskies. Jim and his two daughters Julie and Katie head out with me for at least one evening on the water. It's funny because I fish with the girls and golf with their husbands, as they couldn't care less about muskies. I want to be a good host, so I try to go with the flow. They golf at least 3 days during their stay and starting about 10 years ago they invited me with them. I think they got a kick out of bringing me

An outing with the Gescheidler girls always is memorable and fun. Sue, Mary Beth and Aggie always yuck it up, fish or no fish.

along because I didn't golf worth a poop and I swing a club harder than anyone they ever met. That doesn't mean I have a clue where the ball is headed, but my baseball career in high school and college gave me a swing that is indicative of a caveman. They really love it when I bank a tee shot off the maintenance shed on number eight at the Plum Lake course. The group that week gets a chuckle out of it and we always end up having a fun morning. Sometimes things get a little silly and we end up digging out a potato gun when we get home, making the afternoon interesting as well. This week is a break from fishing and comes at the right time, the middle of the busy summer. I fish only three or four days that week and it is good timing. I'm hungry to get back on the water more because I missed it. It kind of divides the summer up and makes it more manageable.

What The "Pros" Do

I suppose I should define what a "pro" really is in this context. It can be defined as someone who is perceived by the general public as knowledgeable about fishing and can command an audience when he or she talks about angling. I define it as anybody who's in it to make a buck. It could be a writer, a guide, a television host, a bait manufacturer, a tournament angler, or guy with a fancy boat. It is a loose term and no apprenticeship is required. All that is required is that you think you know what you're doing. And, like any other industry, there are the contenders and the pretenders.

Most "pro" fishermen have a network of friends within the industry. They range from other anglers to bait manufacturing reps, to marina operators, to writers. They exchange information about things within the industry to try to better their position in the world. They desire recognition, which leads to higher visibility, which leads to more money. It means paying less for boats and motors. It means getting paid to use certain baits or certain reels.

There are several ways of going about attaining this status. One of the ways is by competing in and doing well in tournaments. This is the most challenging as you are butting heads with other fishermen and proving yourself by being successful in a competitive environment.

Guiding is a way of doing this as well and manufacturers use guides often to help sales by encouraging product recommendations to clients. These clients then run to the shop to get a specific rod and reel combo.

Writers have an "in" on this gravy train as well as the power of the media within their grasp. Whether it is in an article, or an advertisement, a product gets a boost from any kind of exposure and this kind of endorsement can be powerful.

The network that a "pro" develops can be the most important thing that they utilize to improve their standing in the industry. The part of the network that helps them learn about new lakes can be vital.

Many top people within the fishing industry have developed a line of communication with people who manage the fisheries. Fish managers in Ontario, Wisconsin, Minnesota, Michigan, and most other heavy angling states have had contact on a regular basis with guides, writers, and others associated with trying to catch more fish. The goal? Easy. To learn which is the next gold mine to catch big walleyes, trophy bass, and huge muskies. Remember, it's all about where-to. The fish managers are the ones who know what is swimming around out there. It is their job. Their science. The top anglers want to know what they know. They also would like to get these fish mangers drunk, interrogate them, then rummage through their file cabinets looking for fish population estimates on lakes.

The network will also include multi-species anglers who stumble into something great that they didn't anticipate. My favorite thing is when a poor walleye fisherman sees me at a boat launch and he tells me his tale of woe about how all the muskies kept stealing his walleyes as he was reeling them in. I do my best to help him out by getting all those nasty muskies off of his walleye spot. Who says a "pro" isn't willing to help out a fellow angler?

Once these "pro" anglers have an idea about the next location of the "holy grail," they will pound it with the hopes of getting their smiling faces in photographs holding huge fish accompanying an article they wrote about how they caught it. By the time you read about it, and try to figure out where it was caught, the "pro" will be already looking for a new body of water to get more pictures of himself holding up huge fish. It is a vicious cycle and it won't be ending anytime soon. Granted, these "pros" who fish new water get on some wild goose chases, but the "holy grails" they find more than make up for it.

The network of information grows about a certain lake and the "pro" will share data about when and where fish were caught and under what conditions with a select group of people. Information will be exchanged both ways and the "pro" will have the tricks and timing of a lake down to a predictable set of facts. He'll know within a year that if he goes up the 3rd week of June on Lard Lake and the water temperature is over 70 degrees, he will have a good week catching muskies. He must know these types of things because he is counting on the fact that he can go there and catch fish for a client, a photograph, or a video. It's just like Tony Soprano said, "Remember, this is a business."

Secret baits are also a part of the equation. Manufacturers are continually trying to increase sales. They are altering baits in a variety of ways. They add holoform, rubber tails, new propellers, extra blades, new colors, and extra sizes. Some anglers feel like they have to buy it all. (See chapter titled: Why did you buy that?)

Some "pros" will get their hands on a bait prior to it hitting the market. These are called "prototypes" and can make the difference in catching a fish or not. Sometimes a muskie will hit a bait if it is something they haven't seen before. If you have two or three prototypes in your box you can increase the chances of getting the fish to strike. Advantage: "pro."

The bottom line is, making a living in the fishing industry is no easy task. It takes hard work and self-promotion. Modesty is a great thing but not necessarily effective if you want to grow a business. The most successful at this game will look you straight in the eye and tell you exactly how good they are and be willing to jump in the boat to prove it. Walking the walk is simply not enough. Talking the talk draws attention. Attention draws money, and, unlike love, money makes the world go 'round.

The Purpose
Of Tournaments

I was sitting in a classroom during my junior year of college when my professor challenged the class to come up with an idea for a special event for a non-profit organization. I felt this would be simple. At that time, my whole life was a non-profit organization as all revenue was being funneled into pizza, beer, and muskie baits. As groups were assembled within the class to tackle this dilemma, my group was thinking of a variety of things benefiting kids and animals. My mind wandered towards fishing of course, stating that many fishermen are referred to as animals that behave like children. I convinced my group to start a muskie fishing tournament. The benefactor would be a chamber of commerce type organization and the event would be a financial success if it broke even and helped generate revenue in town by tournament anglers patronizing the local businesses.

It's been 15 years since I sat in that classroom dreaming of that event and St. Germain has been hosting the event ever since. The tournament turned a profit immediately and every October some 300 anglers come into town buying gas, renting rooms, eating out, and some even find a way to feed and exercise a few muskies.

This tournament is basically done for fun and there is no real competition for prizes. All the major prizes are given away on a raffle basis. Hopefully this eliminates the need for cheating. The last few years have been different. Muskie tournaments have been set up to mimic the high stakes formats of the walleye and bass fishing world. Tens of thousands of dollars are on the line with the margin sometimes being the fraction of an inch. Have there been problems? A few. Has there been controversy? Yes. Mostly because the people in the muskie world can't seem to agree on what is best for the fish.

The issue of transporting fish from one place in the lake to a holding area is controversial. So is how the fish is either measured or weighed. Some purists don't want tournaments held during warm summer periods when fish suffer more stress in higher water temperatures.

There is a way to use these tournaments as a learning tool. The average fisherman would be able to use the lessons learned both from activity on the water and by watching how these tournament anglers conduct themselves. Some high profile muskie anglers have been involved with tournaments and they sometimes do well. The nature of muskies being what they are however, has let virtually unknown anglers who put in some hard work and imagination rise

Catch and release tournaments have taught a lot of people about specific waters and techniques that work.

to the top. These anglers may not necessarily win consistently, but all you have to be is smarter than the rest of the group for a couple of days and you could walk away with as much as $100,000.

The important thing to remember is that somebody is going to be the best. Pay attention to what they did during their fishing time. Tactics are often revealed upon the completion of the tournament and these tactics can be plugged into that lake on another date to help you catch more fish. This goes for any species including bass, and walleye. Learn from it. Then use it.

As for tournaments, they make money. If they didn't, you wouldn't see so many of them. When you see one being promoted, somebody will be turning some kind of profit from the fishery. If they have a vested interest in the lake and the area that the tournament is being held, you'll know that they don't want to shoot themselves in the foot by hurting the lake. Resorts and homeowners on the lake pay into lake district funds that are used to maintain the health of both the fishery and the water quality. These folks are usually good to their home water. They would be fools to do otherwise.

Looking at tournaments from a guide's perspective is a different matter. Traditionally, guides hate tournaments as they broadcast the success of a particular lake to a large audience. If a guide uses that lake, and a tournament is held there, more people learn the benefits of fishing that water. It also means that during the weekend of a tournament, there will be a higher number of boats out there, keeping a guide from fishing water that he normally might fish. So, some anglers wish tournaments never occur.

If the business of tournament fishing is to be successful, both the anglers and the promoters need to benefit. Small-scale tournaments exist everywhere and help local economies extend their business season by a full extra week in some cases. Large-scale tournaments promote the sport itself, energizing it with new people who will in turn increase the fraternity of fishermen that will make the places that offer these fish vibrant. In this instance, the fish and the lakes are helping people earn their living and allowing them to do it in a beautiful part of the country. Tournaments work.

I Sometimes Cringe While Watching Fishing Shows

It is extremely satisfying to put together a good fishing show because it is not an easy thing to do. I can look at just about every show that I have done and see something that I would like to change or try to improve. It's tough, but when we get a really good segment done, it is a great feeling.

I have seen some great outdoor television. Bucher does a nice job. Mehsikomer has some great shows, so does Flip Palette on Walker's Cay Chronicles. It's work. I appreciate their effort. So, when I see some of the substandard stuff out there, I wonder why they don't try a little harder. The extra effort is worth it.

Camera work is the big thing to look at. It is a visual medium. A shaky camera, an out of focus or dirty lens, or poor lighting is aggravating to watch, especially when you know that these are correctable things.

Sound can be a real tough thing to get just right. Howling winds reek havoc on microphones when you're trying to tape in the elements. Good sound is something you take for granted if you are watching. If you don't have good sound, it is very noticeable and the viewers get frustrated when they watch.

The problem with television however, is that you can have excellent photography, and impeccable sound, but if you have bad subject content or a host that can't speak English the way it was intended, viewers will change the channel very quickly.

The worst program I ever saw was in Michigan around 1993.

Don't Fish Angry

I was on a research trip for Fishing Hot Spots with the head of our research department, Mark Martin. We had checked in at the hotel and were kicking back with a beer when a show came on that I'd never seen before. The host was bear hunting near a state park and the photography and the host's presentation was something out of a 4-H video project. This "host" proceeded to successfully shoot a bear that had been seen in the area. Great. Then it got a little strange. He dragged the bear out to the picnic area of the state park and proceeded to haul this bear (which was slightly bigger than a fat black lab) on to a picnic table and gut it on camera.

Mark and I watched in disbelief as this bumpkin conducted himself like complete pig with terrible on-camera presence and showing inflammatory video such as dressing out a bear on a state park picnic table. I can't imagine the smell that seeped into the wood that the next family enjoyed when they ate off that table.

Another show recently was shot from a bridge over a river and the cameraman simply videotaped anglers who initially didn't know they were ever going to be on a program. Spontaneous? You bet. A good premise for a show? Hardly. By the way, they didn't catch much and the sound of traffic on the bridge made for a nice woodsy, outdoor feel.

There are television programs dealing with the outdoors all over the place. I know several anglers and hunters who appear on these programs and not just the Midwest Adventures program that I host. A chance to appear on a program like this is a great boost for business. My neighbor, Rob Manthei, has appeared on John Gillespie's show as well as ours and he gets a slug of phone calls for guide jobs after he appears. A while back, he caught his largest muskie, a fat 51-incher, on camera with John. Having a great segment like that can really draw attention to you and help increase guide business in the most effective way. The problem is, for every show that features an angler like Rob with a truly big fish like that, there are three shows that deal with some squealing neophyte getting excited about catching 22-inch northerns on a remote fly-in lake in Canada. I see video tape like that more often than I care to see. Now that the cost of broadcast quality cameras has dropped so much over the last 10 years, it seems like anybody can start up a show. Video editing can be done on a PC, eliminating the cost of expensive editing suites. The amount of overhead needed to do a show is so low now that many people are diving into the mix. Some good programming will come out of this flood of new entrants into the race. The competition will force people to eventually improve. In the meantime, be prepared to see some real garbage out there.

There Are More Possibilities Of Failure Than Success

I remember the most depressed I ever felt about fishing. I was in an airplane about 1,000 feet above the Sugar Camp Chain of lakes. It was a beautiful fall day and my Mom, my brother, and I took the fall color ride to see the leaves from the air. I was snapping pictures when I caught a glimpse of a guy in a boat stopping on a familiar shoreline of Dam Lake. As we floated overhead I looked out the window and watched him stand up and throw his first cast. When I saw it land, my heart sank. It was then I realized just how little water is covered with a cast. I could see the entire lake from that plane and he covered about .000000000001% of it with that cast. You have to put that one cast in some pretty special places for it to be successful. I'm glad that the fisherman below me in that boat didn't know what I knew. He was all fired up, ready to set the hook. He was most likely attentive, focused, and expectant of success. But after seeing just how much water you could cover with one cast, for him to hope that he had that bait in front of a fish, I knew he was dreaming. I watched from above as he cranked up his lure and fired his second cast and recognized that failure is a part of fishing.

There are several hundred muskies in a quality lake in our area. That lake could be 1,000 acres. It would have several thousand suckers, shiners, ciscoes, bullheads, bluegills, perch, and minnows. Timing is important. Find this fish when he is hungry. Moon phase, weather change, sunset, or whatever. Just figure it out.

Now, what makes you think that you can find this fish? Find it at the moment he is hungry, and convince him to eat your lure instead of the thousands of other things swimming around that are part of his normal board of fare?

Is it faith? An educated guess? The belief that you can do it no matter what the odds? I guess the answer is yes to all of it. This is why I try to enjoy the journey as much as the destination now. Call it wisdom or the realization that more casts end in failure than with a fish.

I have heard people say that they would trade the big fish that they have caught for the ones they have lost. I suppose I would too. I've hooked some beasts that I couldn't close the deal on. The thing that has changed for me over the years is that when I lose a fish now, I feel more frustration. I want to boat them all.

When I started the muskie game and lost a fish I thought "no problem, I'll just hook another one." Well, after my naiveté wore off, I recognized these things go in streaks and your next chance might be 10,000 casts away, even though I still think that number is crap. Keeping your lure wet is the big thing. I've caught muskies on the

Big fish never come easy no matter what some anglers would have you think.

first cast. I've boated nine in a day. I've caught two muskies on two casts. The only reason I remember these things is because they happen so damn seldom. If you fish enough, freak things will occur like this. A friend of mine once caught sixteen muskies in a day. He only managed to do it the one time though. Does this make him lucky? I say no. He earned them. On that same day he threw approximately 400 casts where not a damn thing happened. Sixteen successful vs. 400 unsuccessful. That is about as good a ratio you can ever hope for. Besides, there were days when this guy threw 600 casts and nothing happened.

A great parallel for muskie fishermen are those who search for sunken Spanish galleons in the Caribbean. There may be the wreck discovery of the century but if you're looking in the wrong place it is never going to be found. Once it's located, you're a millionaire. Well, the muskie world is full of Mel Fischer wannabe's and they all want that huge payday of a monstrous fish. It all comes down to how much are you willing to work to get it.

Working to get yourself in a position to catch a big fish can mean many different things. It may mean driving fourteen hours into Ontario to get to a specific lake. It might mean two men dragging a canoe a half-mile through the woods to get to a lake that has no road or launch on it. It may also mean fishing close to home and paying your dues by catching several small fish and getting a big fish with more effort on water that doesn't have a high density of trophy fish. It can also mean doing a tremendous amount of reading books and surfing the Internet looking for stocking records or lake research information that might clue you in to a good body of water to fish. Work is work. What are you prepared to do once you understand the challenge of catching a big fish?

I guess this is why the nectar of success tastes so sweet. We try and work and toil for the goal of locking horns with the biggest fish in the lake. The hope and expectation can be intoxicating. We know this all when we start fishing at the beginning of the day. Today might be the day. Nonetheless, to this day I try to avoid looking at fishermen when I fly.

How Hollywood
Has Done
Fishing Wrong

O ne of the best movies I've seen about fishing was called
Man's Favorite Sport. It was made in the early 1960's and
stars Rock Hudson as an outdoor writer who masquer-
ades as a fishing expert and wins a large fishing contest out of pure
luck. What makes it so good is that all of the true fishing experts
in the movie are stunned with Hudson's success and his emergence
as a force in tournament fishing from relative obscurity. Aside
from the bimbos that were vying for Rock's attention (who we
now know were wasting their time) the most enjoyable part of the
movie was the deception and secrecy that all parts of the contest
were shrouded in. The methods of catching were secret, the locations were hushed, and the quality of the angler's skills were
absolutely fraudulent. It was fun watching because in the end
Rock Hudson 'fesses up and admits his lies and winds up getting
the girl. (Although we now wonder what he did with her.)

There has been little attention paid to the traditional premise
of fishing in the Midwestern sense of the word. There have been
some great saltwater epics such as Spencer Tracy in The Old Man
and the Sea, Jaws, and The Perfect Storm. Great films with huge
star power and box office punch.

There hasn't been a whole lot of attention paid to our fraternity of angling and it's obviously riveting tales of suspense and raw
sexual energy. There was one stupid slasher type movie filmed in
the Hayward, Wisconsin, area back in the 1980's called Blood

Hook. I paid $4.95 for it on Ebay and I think I got hosed. I look for it to show up on Mystery Science Theatre 3000 any day now.

The closest thing to contemporary reality are the two Grumpy Old Men movies with Jack Lemmon and Walter Matthau. It would figure that the fishing world would rate Sophia Loren and Ann Margaret thirty years after they were something to look at. Those two movies would have been a much better popcorn feed if Kim Bassinger and Jennifer Lopez were trying to seduce those old guys. Just think of the lines that Burgess Meredith would have had for those two!

What we need is for Hollywood to come to a sport show in the winter to do some research for a story of the fishing world. They could meet the players in the industry and try to cast some of roles that are important in the world of fishing.

Ex-boxer Randall "Tex" Cobb could play the role of the helpful game warden. If you can't remember him he was the one that played the bounty hunter in Raising Arizona. A sensitive type who would be an ambassador of goodwill for all that enjoyed the north. Danny DeVito could be the resort owner. Ranting and conniving like he did in Taxi would work well. Gene Hackman could play the corrupt mayor of the quaint resort town. His role as the Sheriff in Unforgiven made me pick him. Jerry Reed could play the owner of the local bait shop. His overall performance as the truck driver in Smoky and the Bandit is enough for me to see on this decision. Jack Nicholson would be the fishing guide. His sincerity and sensitivity towards others is key here. Also we could watch his dementia blossom as he gets closer to Labor Day (see The Shining). He could also tell the client to hold the sucker between his knees (see Five Easy Pieces). Shelly Duvall, the woman who played the wife in The Shining should also play the wife of the guide in this film as well. A gentle loving woman who needs to escape her insane husband by hitting him with a bat, and jumping into a tractor with her family, escaping the remote cold of the north. Chevy Chase would have to be the guide client. His impeccable work in the Vacation movies speaks for itself. His brother in

How Hollywood Has Done Fishing Wrong

law Eddie would have to fish too, metal plate and all. Ned Beatty could play the boat company rep.

Dennis Franz could reprise his role of Sipowitz from NYPD Blue to being an aggressive local fisherman who grills fishing clients on what lakes the guide took them to. He would beat confessions out of them, forcing them to "give it up." He would finish by throwing a legal pad at the sobbing, broken anglers and telling them to write down a list of lakes they fished.

That snotty little kid from the Man Show would be good as the dock boy. Accurate anyway. Dr. Ruth Westheimer should play herself. She should be in every movie stating her case. Maybe she could be the bait shop owner's wife. Leslie Nielsen would be a good choice as the resort bartender. He could give it to you straight (see Airplane). Dennis Hopper could play this role if Nielsen was already booked.

Anna Nicole Smith should probably be in here as well. She needs the work and I think the scenes of her fishing with Jack

Nicholson could provide excellent on-screen chemistry.

We'll also cast "Flipper" here even though this is a freshwater movie. We'll probably have to have that skinny kid from the show as well cause he seems to be the only one who knows what the hell Flipper is talking about. He and the little snot from the Man Show could get together with some bottle rockets.

If you have good characters in the movie, it will be a success. The story would follow the guide throughout the season and culminates as Anna Nicole Smith hires Jack Nicholson so she can win a tournament. She captures Flipper during the contest taking first place. She then horrifies the tournament crowd by devouring Flipper on the dock after accepting her trophy. We could call the movie "Beauty and the Beast" in the most ambiguous way.

Donating Blood
While Fishing

There is a case in an exam room in the emergency department at the Howard Young Medical Center in Woodruff, Wisconsin. It contains hooks of all sizes and each one of them were removed from the flesh of an unfortunate angler who needed help. The sign above this large glass enclosure proudly proclaims the words "People Catchers." I have made a couple of contributions to that board along with thousands of others. Upon completion of hook removal, a nurse then fills out a "People Catcher" card for you with your name on it along with your customer number on it. They start with number 1 at the beginning of every season. In October of 1999, I was angler number 269 to have some embedded steel removed from my hide. That was my most recent trip.

Fishing can be dangerous if you're not paying attention. There are many ways to get hurt. Lightning strikes, pinched fingers, broken bones, concussions, hooks, teeth, gill rakers, sunburn, bee stings, dropped anchors, propellers, carelessness, and stupidity are all common cause for donating blood while fishing. While guiding, there have been few injuries and nothing real serious. For good or bad, most of the time it was me who took the brunt of the punishment.

When I was about thirteen years old, I was hit by a car. It hurt. When I was twenty one, I got hit by an 8-inch Reef Hawg. While the car had more injury potential, I think the Reef Hawg actually hurt more.

It was early in my guiding career and I was fishing for muskies with a fellow from our resort. I was casting just fine on this bright summer day when suddenly everything turned white and I became disoriented. I was kneeling on the floor of the boat and the guest fishing with me was sort of freaking out. It was not until later that I realized I had been hit in the back of the head by his muskie lure. He threw his cast sideways and hit me just above the base of the neck. It really didn't hurt until a few minutes later and the beginning of my four day headache was underway. I could feel a warmth down my back, which turned out to be blood from the gash the bait had caused when I had accidentally been clubbed me like a harp seal. I promptly hung my head over the side of the boat and blew chow. It mixed nicely with my hat, which was also floating in the water. This is an example of how bad casting techniques

Don't be this guy.

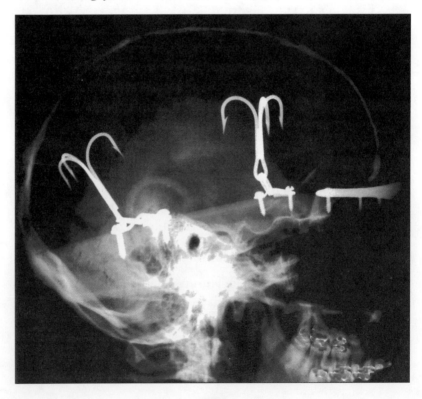

can ruin an otherwise nice day. I was too sick to chew him out. I felt too sick to talk.

After going to the emergency room for a couple of stitches and the doctor telling me a had a slight concussion, I decided that anyone who didn't cast safely in my boat would soon end up on shore. I didn't want to have that happen again to me or anyone else in my boat. As a matter of fact, I have established three simple rules for anybody who fishes in my boat. I tell this to new people when we start out fishing. They are in order of importance:

1. Don't hit me when you're casting.
2. Don't hit anybody else when you're casting.
3. Don't drop any of my stuff into the lake.

That's really all there is. I'm not a mean guy, but I do have standards. Other than those three rules, I'm very flexible.

Bad casting habits or the lack of casting skill is usually the culprit which causes the biggest problems in my boat. I keep a neat boat, watch the weather closely, and usually keep the tomfoolery to a minimum, but an errant cast can happen at any time.

A painful episode happened with an unnamed resort guest a few years back that is indicative of a common problem. Some folks forget to push the casting button on their reel before letting it fly. This guy was casting an 8-inch Swim-Whiz when he forgot to push the magic button. It was a sideswipe job that hit the top of my right hand at a high rate of speed. It hurt like a bitch. Why all the bones in that hand were not crushed I'll never know.

Another fellow with the same flaw in his casting sent a bait for my nether region one summer evening. I saw it coming and actually blocked it with my rod and reel. I lost it a bit with him but he got it together, straightened himself out, and we finished on a good note. He even managed to catch a 41-incher later that same evening.

Hooks and teeth are always a potential problem, especially when dealing with muskies. I have a habit of trying to boat muskies as soon as I can. I don't play them out very long for a couple of reasons. First, the longer you have them on, the greater the chance that you can lose them. Second, the longer you play them, the more exhausted they become and the tougher it is to revive them when releasing. I bring a fair amount of fish into my grasp that have lots of vinegar left in them. Unhooking these creatures and holding them up for a picture can expose an angler to a few dangers if he isn't careful.

The worst I ever received from a fish was eleven stitches in my thumb when I was unhooking a 42-incher in my first tournament. I was digging the hook out of its mouth when it thrashed, driving the hook into my thumb. It was ten seconds of the fish thrashing and shaking before it tore the hook back out. By then I had a nice river of human hydraulic fluid all over the floor of the boat. It was a deep gash, nearly to the bone. Oddly, it didn't hurt much until

Despite friendly service, most customers don't want to repeat their ER visit.

nurse Ratchet shoved a needle full of lighter fluid into it at the emergency room. That hurt worse than the hook. I asked her what that was for and she said it was Novocaine, a local anesthetic. I told her it wasn't working. She smiled slightly and said something in German to Dr. Mengele before he knitted me a new thumb.

I've had to help other boats in some instances when fish were captured and those people did not have the tools, or ability, to unhook a large fish without hurting themselves or the muskie.

My friend Brett Edwards was working the opposite side of a weedbed in Little St. Germain's South Bay with Doug Prigge when I saw Brett hook his first muskie, a handsome 40-incher. They boated the fish, but were struggling with unhooking it. I went over to help and managed to pry the black Suick from its jaws. As I was about to hand the muskie back to him, the fish whirled around and grabbed my right forearm, biting down hard. I was surprised, and instinctively tried to yank my arm straight out, forgetting about the long teeth that were into me.

Luckily, the fish relaxed his grip at the instant I yanked but the fish had done a precise job. The longer teeth on the edge of the jaw had penetrated a vein and a nice mini-geyser of red pumped out of my arm. It only lasted a few seconds, but the blood that escaped coupled with the blood that pooled under the skin made a gunshot wound look more attractive. Brett's fish was released and my arm healed after a few days.

For a few years, I fished with a gentleman from Janesville who made some unique tip-ups for ice fishing. His name was John Rinehart. Now John was as excitable about muskies as anyone I ever met. Until we fished together on a cold November morning a few years back, I did not realize how much he likes to fish.

We set up some tip-ups along a shoreline from our resort where my kind neighbor had one palace of an ice shack. This shack actually sat on the edge of his pier and had electricity, television, heater, pizza oven, and huge picture windows for an awesome view of the fishing area. Six people could fish comfortably in it.

Don't Fish Angry

It was early, a little before 7:00 am when we began to set up and the bait shop wasn't open yet. I set three tip-ups for John which were baited with dead ciscoes and punched three more holes for my tip-ups. I planned to head to the bait shop for some suckers so we would have enough bait for the day. After John was all set, I told him I'd be gone about ten minutes to get bait and I would bring back some coffee and doughnuts. He said that was great and he would get the shack warm.

I went up the hill and stopped at Dave's Landing for the suckers and chewed the fat with Dave a bit. I went next door to the convenience store and bought our healthy breakfast, then drove back to the shack. Total time gone: 15 minutes.

As I walked down the hill I could see that he had a hit. One of the flags was standing tall and was closest to the shack. I picked up the pace going down the steps only to see John half sitting, half lying on the shore looking at the tip up. Something was wrong. "What's going on John?"

With tears starting to form, John gave me a full report. "We have a musky on and I think I broke my ribs!"

"Well John, you've been a busy boy!" I tried to lighten the mood a bit, but he was obviously hurting.

I suggested we pull our lines and go to the doctor. John thought that once the initial pain faded a bit, he could handle it. I cautiously agreed but figured that our day would be cut short. I asked him what in God's name had happened in such a short time.

"You no more than left when one of the flags went off. I was so excited I jumped down the steps onto the glare ice and lost my footing." He slipped and landed on his side and it turned out, cracked a rib on his right side. After a few moments of feeling woozy, he crawled the 100 feet out to the tip-up and set the hook on this fish and fought it to the hole. Realizing it was a musky, he let it swim off figuring he would need some help getting it through the hole onto the ice. Still on all fours and in pain, he crawled back to shore and took up a partial fetal position and waited for my return.

Donating Blood While Fishing

I helped John to his feet and made sure he was going to be able to walk. He replied he felt a little better and wanted to get this muskie onto the ice. We approached the tip-up and John slowly took up the slack. Feeling the fish moving off, he jerked the line and fought the fish back towards the hole after about a 3-minute fight and we got a musky of about 36 inches.

John started to smile a little as we snapped some pictures of the fish and released it. We went back to the shack to take inventory of John's injury.

John had some medication for a different injury up the hill in his truck and that he would give that a try. After all, we caught a muskie after only ten minutes of fishing, and who knows what the day would hold. Besides, we were going to watch the Packer game in the shack and eat pizza while muskie fishing. He wasn't about to miss all that.

John's pain medication seemed to help and he had almost forgotten about the pain by the time the Pack took on Tampa Bay.

Another flag went up and we caught a nice northern but no more muskies. We packed our stuff around 4:00 pm with plans to fish the next day. It would be the last day of muskie season. John seemed OK to walk and move so I figured his ribs would no longer bother him.

The next morning at 6 am I got a call from a very gravelly voiced John Rinehart who said there was no way on earth he was going to be able to fish today. The medication masked the pain while we fished, but once it wore off and he stiffened up in bed that night, he could barely move. He had to cut the trip short and I know that hurt him as much as his ribs.

I fished with John after that but he kiddingly threatened to wear a flak vest like NFL quarterbacks use. He did however, take up the practice of wearing cleats on his boots so he wouldn't lose his footing. To my knowledge, he hasn't fallen again.

Muskie Juice

I'm not sure who started it but around 1960 or so a tradition began at our resort that occurred anytime someone caught a legal muskie. The night they catch the musky, the lucky angler comes up to the lodge and drinks a shot of Platte Valley Corn Whiskey. The person's name and the size of the muskie is written on the bottle. We have many bottles behind the bar at the resort covered with names. Once you catch one here, your name is on the bottle forever.

The youngest person that I'm aware of to down a muskie shot was my brother Tom. He caught his first legal at the ripe old age of ten. I did mine at thirteen and we've had a number of young people boat muskies and do a shot of the vile liquid. All were done with parental consent in the good name of muskie tradition. The only exception made was done recently for a fella who caught two muskies in one evening with me. He was required to do one shot for each fish. The only problem was this guy was a recovering alcoholic. I came up with a perfect solution. I collected up two shot glasses of lake water and made him drink those. His name was written on the bottle with his sobriety intact, and the tradition was not broken.

I was muskie fishing with a couple fellas named Rick and Mike a couple seasons ago and was telling them about our resort's corn whiskey tradition when Rick boated a 35-inch muskie, his first. I informed him that he'll now be a member of the "shot club" when we got back to the lodge.

"How does that stuff taste?" He meekly asked.

"Kind of like feet, except with a lighter fluid aftertaste." My reply.

"Great, can't wait," Rick said, only half smiling.

We hadn't been out much longer when Mike raised a nice muskie on a surface bait. I told him to quit casting and we'll give the fish some time to think about it.

We made a pass over the same weedbed a half an hour later, Rick's surface plug was inhaled by a 41-incher only a few feet from the boat. After a nice fight I lowered my Beckman net into the water and scooped it up.

"HAH! TWO SHOTS OF CORN WHISKEY!!!" I gleefully bellowed while the fish thrashed in the net.

"Hey, ugh! Wait a minute! Isn't it just one shot per person?" Rick looked genuinely worried.

Young Tommy Jackson tries to choke down his first swig of Muskie Juice, a steep price to pay for a 30-incher.

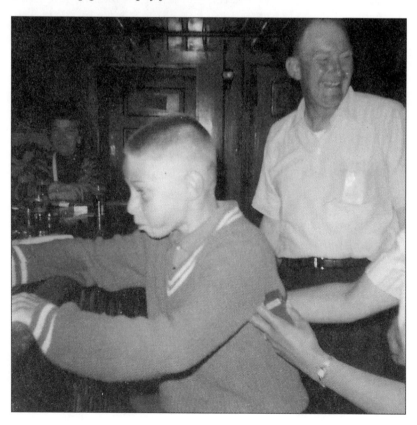

"Sorry man. One shot, one fish. Two shots for two fish." I informed him. His friend Mike was getting a sadistic smile.

The 41-incher was put in the livewell for a little recovery time before photos so we continued up the weed bed. We moved about another 150 feet along the weed bed, then Rick hooked a third fish.

"OH my God! I got another one!" He sounded nervous. I grabbed the flashlight and said something to the effect that Rick must be the thirstiest fisherman on the lake tonight.

I held the net ready and turned on a flashlight. (As it was getting rather dark out by now.) A nice muskie in the 38-inch range came into view as Rick lowered his rod tip and give the fish slack.

"RAISE THE ROD TIP!!!" I hollered at the top of my lungs.

Rick started to shake the rod tip, trying to free the lure from the fish's mouth. He was trying to lose this fish before he had to do three shots of Platte Valley back at the lodge. I reached as far as I could with my net. The muskie was able to shake the hook before I could net it. I looked at Rick and could almost see the wave of relief pass over him as the fish sauntered off back into the cabbage weeds.

I kiddingly let him have it, "You coward."

We all had a good laugh. Most people work their tails off for a muskie and here was Rick, afraid that he actually might get a third one in the same night. I know that corn whiskey doesn't taste like Kool-Aid but I didn't think it was that bad.

When we returned to the dock, his family had a chance to see the 41-incher he caught. After pictures and releasing the fish, I talked to our bartender at the lodge and made sure that he poured two really big shots for Rick. I wasn't going to let him get away with losing the third musky quite so easily.

I advised him that if he loses a fish, he might make it look a little more like an accident than that. Better yet, if anybody balks at the taste, I tell them to just cut their line.

Catching A
Big Fish Can
Be A Headache

I have caught and have guided people to some nice fish. It is a great experience to capture a big muskie or walleye because it is not an easy task. When you catch a "biggie" people envy you and they think you are a good fisherman.

The problem comes when people want to know where you caught it. If you caught it in front of a big group of people, there is little you can do. More often than not though, a big fish is captured with little fanfare and the anglers themselves are in a position to say how much they want to about its size and capture. Most of these anglers want to draw little attention to what lake they were fishing and do not want to bring more pressure to a body of water they care about. They talk about how they caught it, not where.

Another problem that comes with catching a big fish is envy. Other anglers are not always happy if you catch a big fish, especially if you've caught big ones in the past. Sometimes other anglers will do their best to dispel the size of the fish or how it was caught in a way to lessen the accomplishment of the catch.

The practice of catch and release has complicated this situation even more. The fact that you can claim the size of the fish without having to produce the fish can make things even more questionable. Polaroid photographs can be some proof but looking at a man that is holding a 47-inch muskie and another man that is holding a 49-inch muskie can be easy to mix up. This is

Don't Fish Angry

especially true if the man holding the shorter fish is 5' 10" and the one with the longer fish is 6' 3" and weighs 35 pounds more.

Some anglers who have caught muskies of giant proportions have been subjected to some harsh questions and scrutiny even though some of these fish have been caught legitimately and within the bounds of good sportsmanship. Some anglers can't stand to see another guy succeed. These are fish that exceed 51 or so inches and blow through the magical 40-pound mark. These are rare fish and only a handful are captured across the Midwest and Canada each year. Some of these colossal fish are even scrutinized if they are kept and shown on display, the nay-sayers claiming either questionable angling methods or a scale giving incorrect weight measurements. The bottom line is, if it seems too good to be true, the thought is that somebody must have cheated.

I know a story about a Canadian resort owner who intentionally said a fish was about 3 inches shorter than it actually was. The reasoning was the size of the fish was more believable and he didn't want the headache of having to prove the size of a released muskie. He knew it was a big fish and he thought he would let the pictures of the fish speak for itself. A truly unfortunate situation.

The recent scrutiny over world records being questioned has been bordering on the ridiculous. Our generation has been practicing a fair amount of revisionism and it stands to reason that jealousy and lack of faith have something to do with it. The fact is that fisherman, for the most part, are an honest group. There were liars in the old days, and liars that exist today. Is it the majority? I think not. Should we try to change the past that is impossible to verify? Why bother? I will tell you why. It's because every good fisherman thinks the world record fish could be out there and may be within their grasp. It is time to catch the new world record.

Eight-year-old Thelma Jackson poses with a muskie reputed to be 50 pounds captured in September 1913. The fish was later discovered to be 43 pounds.

Don't Fish Angry

The best way to handle this whole situation is to go out on the morning of July 4th and catch an immense muskie from a bridge that is jammed with holiday traffic. Have a 10,000 gallon glass tank ready to throw the muskie in, and tow it down the parade route on Main Street during the July 4th celebration so thousands of people could witness it. When the tank reaches the post office, grab the beast from the tank and club it over the head with a 55-gallon barrel, then drag it across the parking lot into the post office so it can be weighed accurately. After tipping the scale at 81.25 pounds, the fish can then be displayed out in front of the town hall in a satin-lined casket under a huge tent so other anglers could file past and pay their respects. The fish can then be fitted for a glass mausoleum and you could hire a mortician to handle the embalming. Maybe we could call Russia and get the guy who did the Lenin job. He's been pickled for years and still looks healthy and tanned. Anyway, the fish would be on permanent display so some clown 50 years from now couldn't come down and say that the fish should be questioned on its verified weight.

I Laughed
So Hard
I Cried

Husband and Wife Clients

There are some guide jobs that stand out. They are interesting from the moment the client calls the house to book the day. A woman who was fairly forward called and said that she wanted to book a day of fishing. She and her husband were coming up to visit our neck of the woods and decided to hire a guide and catch a batch of panfish. After talking to her on the phone a couple of times, I could tell she was a woman who was pretty self-sufficient. I also discovered that whenever she talked, she sucked all the oxygen out of a room. When I met these folks for our trip, I saw her poor husband had been worn down by the years. His most repeated phrase over the decades must have been "Yes, dear." She did 97% of the talking in that marriage.

Over the course of our morning, she gave out her various opinions on several subjects and both her husband and I sat and listened. Me out of politeness and him from just calling it another day since the wedding.

We had caught a nice number of perch and crappies and it was getting time to call it a morning. I was glad because this woman's constant prattling was starting to give me a rash. We were in the last spot and I suggested that we should make two more casts and then head back to the pier. Just then, she set the hook and the rod bent quite hard. I did not see the rod tip bounce like a fish was on. She continued to hold heavy pressure on the rod. She was still talking non-stop and now commenting on the fish she was about to bring in. Suddenly, the rod flattened out and a large gob of weeds came free with her jig. The whole works came flying towards the boat. She was in mid-comment when the weeds were

inbound and her husband and I watched as the gob of slimy brown weeds hit her in the mouth during her monolog. I was worried that the jig may have hit her face but she seemed all right other than the unwanted salad bar she had caught in her pie hole. It was across her nose and she was spitting out pieces of weed. I felt badly for her, as this was a bit of a mess. It was then a chuckle came from the bow of the boat. This chuckle was the first sign of emotion her husband had displayed the whole trip. It caught me off guard and I started to laugh myself.

She whirled around and shot him a nasty glare. He quieted down, but I had a tough time keeping it in. I said to both of them that we should probably end on that note and she agreed, still wiping the mess from her face. I turned away from them, trying not to laugh while putting away tackle and pulling up the anchor.

On the way back to the pier, I kept thinking of anything I could to keep the vision of this woman with a mouthful of weeds out of my head but it was too funny. I kept thinking of the joy her husband must have felt watching this fleeting moment of humor. There were many times that he may have wanted to shove something into her mouth to shut her up. Fate intervened for him and she did it to herself. I was glad when they got out of the boat because I could not hold it any longer. As I headed back to the launch, I let go and laughed so hard I could barely drive the boat.

Eastern Bloc Muskie

It was a late August afternoon and we had about six cottages with people. It was a slow week with not as much fishing at the resort. There was a young family from Racine and also a couple of cottages of people from the Chicago area who had immigrated from Latvia, which had been part of Eastern Europe. These folks came to relax and walk through our woods picking mushrooms and enjoying the peace and quiet of the north. They were very nice people with heavy accents but spoke excellent English.

I had a good streak of muskies going that week and came across an evening when I wasn't scheduled to guide. I still wanted to fish though and went down to the cabin with the young family and asked the husband if he wanted to join me for a few hours that evening. He was enthusiastic about going. I told him to meet me by the lodge at 6:00 pm.

I was in front of the lodge at quarter-to-six when the man came over and I could tell something was amiss. He had a long look on his face and said that he had to cook burgers on the grill and that the family wanted to eat together. He had been shot down and was not happy about missing a muskie outing during a week that I was on the fish.

Since I was packed up and ready to head out, I decided to wander over to one of the other cabins that had some of our friends from Latvia. I knocked on Naum Fertilmeister's door and asked him if he wanted to give muskie fishing a shot. He checked with Mrs. Fertilmeister and she said they could eat a late supper and she would read a book while he was gone. So, Naum and I headed to the bait shop to get a fishing license.

We went to Big St. Germain that evening and I had to show Naum how to cast and retrieve the bait properly. He was learning from scratch and I asked him how much fishing he had done when he was younger. I think he told me that night it had been thirteen years since he had gone out or even tried to catch a fish. I wondered how this guy would handle a muskie if it hit.

We were on the water for only 45 minutes when we pulled up to the weedbed off of Lynn Ann's campground and started to work the edge of the weeds. I had Naum throwing a Tallywacker surface bait while I threw a bucktail. I was watching my lure coming in when a huge geyser of water shot up next to the boat in front of Naum. A nice muskie decided to hit his surface bait with about 18 inches of line out. It cartwheeled next to the boat like it was an Olympic gymnast. Naum started freaking out, but in Latvian. Vlodastabuk! Hollistania! Ug! Vodka! This went on for about ten seconds. I guess when you are flipping out and don't know what to do, you revert back to your home language.

Once I realized Naum was into a nice fish, I cranked my bucktail in as fast as I could so I could help him. He was fighting this fish with less than 3 feet of line out and there was so much pressure on the line he was unable to push the free spool button and give the muskie some line to work with. Meanwhile, the muskie was being as violent as it could possibly be, along with a wigged out Latvian on the other end of the line. I'm not sure who was fighting whom.

I had to make a split second decision and it paid off. Instead of trying to coach Naum though this chaos, I grabbed the net and took a wild stab at the muskie during the fierce gyrations and scored with a mid-air scoop job. From hook set to

Naum survives his boatside battle with this 42-incher long enough to pose for this photo.

netting, the entire fight was no more than fifteen seconds. Naum collapsed in his seat and was breathing as though he had run a sprint. I was rattled because Naum squared off with this fish and cursed it like a KGB agent with an expired visa.

After the dust settled, we looked at each other and laughed. I hung onto the net handle and held the bag in the water while we peered over the side and looked at Naum's first fish, a handsome 42-inch silver muskie. He was shaking too much to hold it for a picture, so I decided to put the muskie in my livewell and find someone to take a picture of both of us with the fish. This way I could hold it for him. We found a cabin on shore with lights on and interrupted a card game so a lady could come down to her dock and take the picture for us. I talked Naum into releasing his fish and we would have photos to remember the moment. By the time we released the fish, it was dark and I thought it would be smart to head back home. Naum had a tough enough time fighting a muskie when we could see. I didn't want to know what would happen if he hooked one in complete darkness.

We arrived back at the cabin well after dark, triumphant from the victory of Naum's first muskie. His wife asked where it was and he told her about releasing it. She seemed to doubt the story until I backed it up. Naum was recounting the story of the epic battle when the young family man that had to take part in the family barbeque strolled over to see what the commotion was all about. This poor guy had to listen to Naum's account of the epic battle and the excitement that we had experienced. Naum had basically caught what could have been his fish, had it not been for his family barbeque duties.

Naum went to the lodge that night and downed his shot of the muskie juice and we put his name on the bottle. For the rest of my life, I will remember the string of foreign obscenities that Naum blurted out in his moment of terror, as he stared into the face of the angry muskie that struck next to the boat.

What Are You Fishing For With That Sucker?

When you fish lakes with a lot of tourist activity, you're bound to see quite a few bizarre and funny things. Take for instance the day Ty Prigge and I were fishing the area near the Tobin Bar on Little St. Germain Lake.

I had been seeing a number of nice muskies in the area, but the Tobin Bar is by no means a secret spot on Little Saint. It has produced many large fish over the years. If you are fishing on a Sunday afternoon like Ty and I were, you are bound to share it with a few other folks.

We were drifting out on the weed edge when I began watching this one old Starcraft boat with a couple of anglers fishing way too shallow. They had heavy musky rods and massive bobbers all over the place. They looked like they were after catfish or something. They were after muskies but from the looks of their situation, they would have settled for just about anything. About the time I saw these fellas, I also noticed a large bald eagle flying overhead not far from the Starcraft. I recognized this eagle immediately because it had a small section of feathers missing from its left wing. This bird had been flying around our lake most of the summer.

The farther up the weedbed that we drifted, the more Ty and I noticed this bird getting closer to this other boat. I was surprised at how close it was circling to them. I got Ty's attention just in time for him to see this bird slam its talons into the water no more than 15 feet from their boat and come up with a nice sized fish. It made one helluva splash.

The guys in the Starcraft were oblivious to this bird and it's circling. They were casting downwind and not even looking toward where the bird was. It was about then that I saw one of the fellas get all excited and run towards the back of the boat reaching through all the tackle and nets in the boat to grab one of their rods. He apparently had a strike. I could see there was a rod jumping and shaking and I could hear the bait clicker going like mad.

This guy was pretty keyed up and grabbed the rod when I saw this horrified look on his face like he didn't know what to do. I glanced up and I saw the eagle that had just grabbed this fish with a huge beach ball-sized bobber dangling below it as it flew off towards the north. The eagle had grabbed this guy's musky sucker. Ty and I started to laugh so hard that tears were running down our faces. Here was this poor oaf from out of town probably hoping for the fish of a lifetime and now he's all set to do battle with not the state fish but the national symbol!

The other fella in the boat ran back to help his buddy but there wasn't much that he could do. At least the man with the rod had the good sense to not set the hook. The eagle kept flying and actually gained altitude and speed with his nice big dinner in tow, bobber hanging below him, as he sailed over the trees, stripping every inch of line off this poor man's reel.

It was about this time that Ty and I were catching our breath from laughing at these poor guys and their unusual situation. They no doubt heard our laughter, as they quietly cranked up their remaining lines and quickly exited the Tobin Bar. I'm not sure if they ever came back.

The eagle survived the incident. Approximately three days later I saw the same eagle (with distinct feathers missing from the one wing) in the area of the Tobin Bar. He was flying with no problems and landed in a large white pine tree with no ill effects. He saw no boats trailing suckers and left the area immediately.

Boats:
The Good, The
Bad, & The Ugly

I used to be emotional when it came to boats. I could understand the reasoning behind naming a boat and calling it a home on the water. Now, to me, boats are merely a tool and the function that they serve is more important than any warm fuzzy feeling it can provide.

The boat needs to do the job, look good, and be easy to maintain. It must offer durability, plenty of space, and provide safety under rough conditions. Guiding is a job. Like any job, you need a workspace. That is how much romanticism exists between me and my boat. I also often sell my boat after each season so I no longer have it long enough to get attached to it.

What most guides need is two boats, at least in my neck of the woods. One boat is for muskies and the other boat is for every other fish. The reasoning behind this is that muskie tackle is so heavy, and you need so much of it, that you end up loading and unloading what seems like a half ton of crap each time you switch species. There are tackle boxes, rods, tools, and a net that an eight year old child could fit into. There are many boxes and they are all heavy.

When dealing with tackle for other fish, there are also many boxes and they are almost as heavy. For bass, you'll need several rods, boxes of plastics, jig heads, crankbaits, weights, and plenty of little doo-dads to make these fish hit. Walleyes require tons of tackle. You'll need planer boards, rod holders, crankbaits, jigs (different than the bass jigs), rods for jigging, slip bobbering, trolling with leadcore line, flatline trolling, bait rigging, bottom bouncing, and crankbait casting. Your net should have a handle about six feet long as well. If you are truly serious about fishing, you have to do some loading and unloading of this massive pile of equipment if you target multiple species. Just have a good chiropractor on speed dial.

It can be difficult for me when fishing in someone else's boat. I feel obligated to bring along so much of my own stuff because I can't anticipate what the other boat has for standard equipment. I bring a scary amount of tackle along due to the fact that I am insecure. I can't get caught on the water without a certain group of "core" baits that generally produce for me. I always bring a few extra items as well.

Boats are a source of worry for me as well. Because I sell my boat at the end of each season, I'm forever concerned about scratches and scrapes that naturally occur if you use a boat as much as I do. When approaching a dock I've got my bumpers out and I play the wind as carefully as I can when pulling up. I hate the sound of the metal edging scratching the hull. It's worse than fingernails on a chalkboard.

My biggest problem about boats is that I only seem to like the expensive ones. After guiding this long and fishing as much as I have, the features of the economical boats just don't fit the bill for my kind of fishing. Now at least, my vehicle is worth more than my boat. It wasn't always that way. I suppose that is a criteria for the "bubba" factor. If your boat is worth more than the truck pulling it, perhaps you truly are a redneck.

Dogs
In The Boat

Growing up in the Jackson house meant that you were a dog lover. My mom always had a soft spot for canines, especially black labs. We had a number of mixed breeds, but they usually had some type of lab or retriever blood line in it. Being a family that lived on the lake and fished, you had to know that dogs were going to be fishing right along with us. They loved to face the bow at full speed, the wind blowing their ears around like streamers on a parade float. I can almost picture Jacques, our big yellow lab from the early 1980's, in the bow almost smiling as the breeze traveled over him while we raced between fishing spots.

Dogs, however, had more shortcomings in the boat than benefits, especially the dogs we had when I was growing up. Jag, Sassy, and Jacques were a few of them. My Dad had a soft spot for one of our dogs from many years ago, a mixed breed aptly named "Klutz." I'm not sure how many rod tips that dog snapped off, but it apparently didn't frustrate my Dad enough to leave him on shore. Klutz had a tough time finding a comfortable spot in the boat and wouldn't settle down. He was constantly pacing over the seats and was always moving. He would step on a rod tip or do something that earned him his name that would garner a yell from my Dad. Jacques' shortcoming was that he was just too big, especially in a small boat. Being over 100 pounds, Jacques would constantly be in the way and feel obligated to paw at you and want to play when I was jigging for walleyes.

My Mom's dog for many years, a nervous lab named "Curley," crossed the line. That dog actually cost me a nice muskie. Curley wasn't the most affectionate dog but it was the dog of the house at the time and I tried to make peace with it. I figured if the dog went on a boat ride, she would settle down and maybe lighten up a little when I entered a room.

We had fished a couple of places for muskies and pulled up to our last spot of the evening, the Lang Bar. My red bucktail was coming in parallel to the weed edge when I caught a glimpse of a nice green missile chasing it. The dog saw the fish following and tilted its head as the fish started to turn while I performed a figure-eight with my bucktail. I made five or six turns with the bucktail when the water finally erupted, showering both Curley and me. Curley recoiled in terror and backpedaled to the bow, knocking over a plastic bait pail that had several other muskie baits hanging from it. The dog was startled by the bucket and knocked it around even more, spreading several baits with big hooks all over the deck. Meanwhile, I have a 20-pound class muskie standing on its tail right next to the boat.

I saw Curley's predicament and envisioned one of my hooks ending up in the dog's foot and me taking this quivering black animal to the vet that night to harvest a bait from its paw. This scenario distracted me from my main job, catching this fish I so dearly wanted. The muskie wasn't hooked very well, so I would have to be patient in getting it in a position to net it. In my hopes of settling both the muskie and the dog down, I was distracted and ended up putting too much back pressure on the fish. This caused it to jump high into the air, throwing the bucktail back at me in disdain.

I eyed the dog and Curley seemed to realize the mood in the boat had changed. I was no longer willing to work at being this dog's buddy. I quietly picked up the loose baits, flung them into the bucket, and fired up the motor to head back to the resort. Curley never set foot in my boat again.

It was not long after that debacle when a stray dog wandered into our resort on a warm September afternoon. He was good natured, medium sized and seemed housebroken. Having no collar or tags, we wondered who he belonged to and where was his home. After a couple of days of inquires, we found no owner and I thought I would put this dog to the test. How good was he in a boat?

I invited him in and he immediately went to the bow and let his ears flap in the wind. He reminded me of Jacques right away, only smaller. I stopped in the West Bay Narrows and started to throw a Suick. On my sixth, cast I felt a welcoming jolt and soon a plump 37-incher was resting in my net. I glanced up to see what

Dogs enjoy angling for walleyes as much as muskies.

the dog was up to and he could barely keep his eyes open. He was sleeping on the front deck and hardly noticed the fight of the fish and couldn't care less. This was a good thing I thought, still feeling the sting of the outing with Curley not long before. A muskie his first time out and he sleeps in the bow.

I switched spots after releasing that muskie and was in deep water throwing a Cisco Kid for suspended muskies when I decided that I needed to keep this dog. Just then, a group of ciscoes broke the surface near the boat and I looked at the dog and decided that was it. His name is Cisco. While this was an important moment for me (I had never named a dog before), it still looked like he could barely keep his eyes open. I could have named him "toilet brush" and it would have been all the same to him. But, Cisco fit and he has been by far the best dog for fish karma and good behavior. The name was also appropriate because he sometimes comes home smelly and slimy like a fish.

His affection has sometimes been inconvenient, as he has tracked me down on the lake when I went fishing without him. The first incident was only a few weeks after I acquired him. I was guiding on Little St. Germain and working the shoreline in front of my Mom's house. Cisco must have heard my voice because he came barreling down the hill and jumped into the lake. He swam out to the boat, much to the disbelief of my clients. I pulled the sopping wet dog aboard and, of course, he proceeded to shake, covering my clients with spray on a brisk October afternoon. I had to pause the guide trip for a few minutes while I hauled my wet hound up the hill and tied him up at Mom's house until I could get back.

He truly proved his stamina another time, chasing me down in a canoe near the Sunken Island, nearly a quarter of a mile from the resort. I would have invited him along as I was alone, but he seemed occupied with a chipmunk that he was tormenting. While I was casting, I could hear him wheezing as he approached from the distance. It was a mastery of balance and physics pulling a 50-pound, sopping wet dog aboard a canoe without flipping it.

Dogs In The Boat

Luckily for me, he has mellowed with age but he still likes to ride. Plus, his fish karma is still pretty good.

Cisco demonstrates his fish karma is good on the ice as well as in the boat.

Weather

I don't want to admit to foolish behavior here, but I have been close enough to lightning bolts to smell the burnt wood from the tree it struck. Nobody intentionally puts themselves at risk, but it really isn't until you get the hell scared out of you that you truly respect the power of something.

I was always careful about electrical storms because of a run through the woods I made when I was nine years old. The school bus dropped me off at a certain spot every day and I had to walk the remainder to get home. I ran almost a half-mile through the woods one day during a powerful lightning storm when several ground strikes happened. It never kept me up at night, but I can still remember the horrible sound that a lightning bolt makes when it sizzles over your head, just before the thunder booms. It dominates your eardrums until you think it will never stop. I'm careful and you should be too.

I tell my clients or anyone else who fishes with me that I'll fish in a snowstorm, but lightning is something I won't mess with. There are instances where I was caught unaware that a storm was approaching, but I have gotten better at anticipating that sort of trouble.

When getting caught off guard by the weather, it is usually because you traveled too far away from the resort or dock. My friend Rick Mai and I were about six miles from our resort on the Winnipeg River and we were distracted by the muskies we were catching. Rick and I had put three muskies in the boat that day that were 40, 42, and 48 inches. The two of us were on a roll and the last thing we were worried about was the weather.

Rick had just released the 40 incher when we rounded the tip of a large island. It was a typical island on a Canadian Shield lake, with a massive rock cliff, and jutted high out of the water. When close to the island, like we were, there was almost no visibility of the distant western sky. When I caught a glimpse of the sky past the island, I knew we were in for a rough ride.

The sky was black like soot and I could see lightning coming down out of the darkest parts. The distant thunder had been muffled by the island and the sound of the outboard as we trolled. We were close to it now, though.

I fired up the engine and pointed the bow towards the storm. We had to go through it to get back to camp. As the boat got on plane, lightning struck an island about a half-mile in front of us. Rick took his 6-foot-4-inch frame into a crouched position in the bow. As we went deeper into the storm with the sharp lightning and thunder, Rick became even smaller. By the time we approached the island that had just been struck, Rick looked about as big as Gary Coleman.

This is a sign you stayed out a half hour too long.

Don't Fish Angry

The toughest part by now was the rain. The biggest raindrops I had ever seen were hitting me in the eyes and it was tough to see. The rain even stung my bare hand as I twisted the throttle on the tiller handle. The lightning was almost constant and appeared in three different forms. There was the ground strike, of which I had seen three by the halfway point to camp. There was what I call spider web lightning. It is lightning that travels on the underside of the cloud and stretches out for miles, looking like a web of blue fire in the sky. This was the spookiest. That lightning made it seem like nothing was out of its reach. Third was the bright, general flash. This was tough because it was directly overhead and the thunder came at the same time. This was the one that scared the hell out of me. I couldn't tell if it was a ground strike right next to me.

I kept wondering if we were doing the right thing. Should we beach it and get on an island or run for home? I kept seeing these islands getting nailed by voltage from the sky and decided to keep going. It probably lasted only twelve or thirteen minutes, but that was the longest boat ride of my life.

We arrived at the dock at camp and, although the rain was still severe, the lightning started to let up almost as we hit the pier. Both of us left our gear in the boat. I pushed the bilge pump switch and headed for the cabin. Two of our other fishing partners, Rob Manthei and Ty Prigge, were dry, relaxed, and surprised to see us. Each had a beer. They wondered what the big deal was. I said nothing. I walked over to the cabinet, pulled out a bottle of V.O. and poured half a water glass full. My hand was still shaking slightly. I drank it in three gulps and sat down. I looked at Rick and he looked at me, laughing. We admitted to each other later that we were scared shitless. Being prepared for a day like that is not tough — just wear the best rain suit with a grounding rod and you're all set.

The fall can be tough due to the changes that can occur. A warm morning can turn into a cold afternoon and vice versa. The biggest mistakes I see clients make is that they are not prepared for the weather. Especially cold weather. They do not seem to realize that the temperature on land is about 10 degrees warmer than on the water. The wind isn't as evident on land either. I can often tell early in the morning if the people in my boat are dressed right for the day. I can almost predict a client calling it early due to self-imposed hypothermia. It's a shame too. Some big fish can be caught on cold days if you're ready for it.

Fish react to millions of different stimuli. The weather can be one of the strongest influences that make fish do what they do. Warm fronts are good. Cold fronts are bad. Stable weather helps. Most of the guides I know subscribe to these basic theories. But, each angler has caught fish under bad weather conditions and these are the times that a guide truly earns his pay. Any shmuck can be a guide when the fish are biting well. If you can make

After Rick released this 40-incher, I had the longest 12-minute boat ride of my life. Though this picture appears to have been taken at night, it was shot in the middle of the afternoon in a driving rain-storm.

chicken soup out of chicken shit though, you are a special breed. You're also most likely anal about keeping records about weather conditions and have made connections with specific lakes under those conditions.

I have a favorite condition for fishing on each specific lake. Because of this, I consider the weather before I pick the lake. It is only one of the factors, but it is an important one. Most guides use this approach if they are in a region that has many different lakes as in Northern Wisconsin. If a guide stays on one specific water such as Lake of the Woods or Mille Lacs, they probably have specific sections of the lake that they concentrate on most during specific weather patterns. It makes sense to keep track of these things. This makes the process of finding active fish simpler the next time Mother Nature throws you a curveball.

There are also times when fishing seems like the thing only foolish people do. My extremes of weather range from a day in June of 1995 when I was muskie fishing with the Steinbrecher family in 103-degree heat. I also think back to November of 1991 when I put my boat in on Big St. Germain and the temperature that morning was 4 degrees above zero. The 48-mph winds on the Chippewa Flowage with Dave Dorazio were quite refreshing. The eight inches of snow in my boat when I took Tim Orr walleye fishing in May of 1997 were memorable as well. All of these situations were instances when I could have talked these people into staying in that day but we decided to try it anyway. Some of these trips were worth it, the others were a waste of time. The point is that before you go, you can't be sure of what will happen. The day you pick might be the best day of the year. It might be the worst day. You have to go out and give it an honest shot. Remember, you can't catch a fish if you are sitting on a bar stool.

Final Thoughts About The Guide's Experience

I f you've made it this far, you have probably concluded that being a fishing guide requires you to have a screw loose. It doesn't pay that well, the hours are long, and success is not even close to a guarantee. It is a labor of love. Most of the guides I know are smart, hardworking sportsmen who have a passion for nature and have sworn to an unwritten oath that charges them with educating people about the outdoors. It is the responsibility of the guide's client to try to learn as much as possible and carry with him or her the lessons of the day that you spent together. The fish are just a small part of the experience. The trees, birds, flowers, lakes and various wildlife are there for the taking as well. Make sure that you don't forget to experience all of it.

Before we learned how to troll with planer boards, or probe the thermocline, or run a GPS unit, we were simple fishermen. We grew up fishing with our brothers and fathers and enjoyed the uncomplicated pleasures of catching fish because it was fun. I won't pretend to speak for all fishing guides but I am sure many would agree with me. Even though it is now a business, we try to pass on that same fun for others. That makes the experience for us worth all the effort.

Thanks, Dad

About The Author

Ken Jackson grew up on the shores of Little St. Germain Lake in Vilas County, Wisconsin, at Jackson's Lakeside Cottages, a resort built by his great-grandfather.

Ken started guiding at the age of 19, though he fished with resort guests since his father let him run a boat. He has written for *Musky Hunter* magazine, the *Lakeland Times* and various other outdoor publications.

In 1999 he became technical producer of the outdoor television show, Midwest Adventures. His fishing travels have taken him to Ontario, Minnesota and Michigan, as well as his home waters in northern Wisconsin.

Ken and his wife, Linnea, have two children. They reside on the same land that his great-grandfather purchased in 1921.

Over the years he has learned to not fish angry.